RICK RO

Foreword by Rick Steves

A JOURNEY CALLED HOPE

TODAY'S IMMIGRANT STORIES AND THE AMERICAN DREAM

Advance Praise for *A Journey Called Hope*

"In his beautiful story sharing, Rick Rouse humanizes the refugees who are often just seen as numbers or political pawns in this country. I am grateful for his diligent work recounting the ways that refugees are hopeful, beloved, and kind neighbors who ought not to simply be welcomed here, but who deserve to be recognized as essential to our national identity and the rich blessing of a diverse life shared with all of God's children. I thoroughly enjoyed reading Rick's writing and recommend it to anyone willing to have their horizons expanded, eyes opened, and hearts filled with new, or renewed, passion for refugee welcome in this country."

— *Alan Dicken, Associate Director for Immigration and Refugee Response, Christian Church (Disciples of Christ)*

"*A Journey Called Hope* reminds us of the often unfulfilled promise of America to be a haven and home for those seeking safety and hope. Immigration reform remains a challenge, and the first order of business is to agree that our promise can only be fulfilled by acknowledging the extraordinary contributions that immigrant communities have made, and fully affirming their humanity and right to flourish. If America is to be what we say we are, we must listen the words of Rouse and others who call us forth to fulfill this promise of safety and hope for all."

— *Rev. Teresa "Terri" Hord Owens, General Minister and President, Christian Church (Disciples of Christ) in the United States and Canada*

"*A Journey Called Hope* is very important for our time. The book is grounded in impressive research, and the conclusions are incredibly clear and coherent. I also liked the reflection questions at the end of each chapter, which are perfect for small groups or individual study. Rouse has written a book about a timely subject that the entire American Church needs to focus on in adult education and preaching. I also think non-church people will benefit from reading this book."

— *Paul Ingram, Professor Emeritus, Pacific Lutheran University*

"If you are wondering why you would want to hear yet another point of view about the contested debate this nation is having about immigration, consider opening your heart to the stories of those wandering the earth in search of home and life. In this inspiring and hopeful book, Rick Rouse sets the stage with a brief and challenging history of immigration in America and then invites the reader to accompany these sojourners as fellow human beings, in the hope that the fear, blame, and dehumanizing rhetoric driving this crisis can give way to empathy and appreciation of their dignity and our shared humanity. These stories dispel the caricatures of immigrants and refugees and reveal the depth of their character and courage. They also raise the question of who we are as part of the one human family and what we want to become as nation."

— *Ray Pickett, Rector, Pacific Lutheran Theological Seminary*

"Humanizing immigrants and refugees by allowing them to tell their own stories is a critical step toward winning greater acceptance of those who contribute to the greatness of our country. I am grateful that Rouse has brought their stories to life."

— *Beto O'Rourke, former U.S. Representative to Congress, Sixteenth Congressional District of Texas*

"In Matthew 25, Jesus provides criteria for how the nations will be judged: Did you feed the hungry? Did you clothe the naked? Did you care for the sick? Did you visit those in prison? Did you welcome the stranger? In this book, Rick Rouse calls our nation to account for how we either do or do not welcome the stranger. And in doing so, he gives a message of hope: not only is that the right thing to do, not only is it good for the refugee and for the migrant, it also makes our nation a better place. Moreover, for the individual Christian, Jesus tells us that welcoming the stranger is one of the ways in which we can come closer to following our Lord. As our nation goes through a time of political polarization and fear-mongering, this is a book of hope—and inspiration."

— *Ralston Deffenbaugh, President of Lutheran Immigration and Refugee Service (1991–2009) and the Lutheran World Federation's Assistant General Secretary for International Affairs and Human Rights (2010–2017)*

"*A Journey Called Hope* arrives at a critical time for our nation and communities. Rick Rouse has done an extraordinary job succinctly tracing the history of how America has extended welcome to newcomers and doesn't shy away from the challenges. At the same time, he lifts up the powerful stories and experiences of some of these new neighbors and calls us to reflect on their journey and our own. Read this book and discuss the accompanying questions in your book group, class, church, or on your own. Now is the time for a well-informed national conversation on these issues."

— *Linda Hartke, Past President, Lutheran Immigration and Refugee Service*

"This engaging and timely book introduces us to immigration and to immigrants. *A Journey Called Hope* seeks to overcome our society's pervasive fear and misinformation about immigration. It clarifies what's at stake and introduces us to the experiences of individual immigrants. Our history is checkered. At times, some immigrants have been welcomed. At other times, various groups have been excluded. Now is a time to welcome immigrants, because people are being displaced from their homes at an alarming rate, because our country will benefit from their presence, and [because] the biblical tradition joins with our nation's ideals to urge welcoming and aiding today's strangers/immigrants.

— *Darrell Jodock, Professor Emeritus, Gustavus Adolphus College*

"'I was a stranger and you welcomed me ...' In Part One of *A Journey Called Hope*, Rouse explores the history and today's landscape of immigration law and the policies and practices of the United States. In Part Two, we are privileged to read rich, beautiful, and ultimately hopeful stories of immigrants who traveled far to come to America. In Part Three, these two sections are woven together as Pastor Rouse lifts a vision of hope through God. I am grateful for this book, and encourage individuals, congregations, and other communities to engage in the questions at the end of each chapter as we join in God's vision: To welcome, to journey, to work to change systems that harm, and ultimately [to] join together with God in holy community."

— *Bishop Shelley Bryan Wee, Northwest Washington Synod of the Evangelical Lutheran Church in America*

"If you need a hopeful word about the current state of immigration, *A Journey Called Hope* will introduce you to the face of immigration. Rouse shares a compelling story of the human beings caught up in global displacement. He doesn't dwell on statistics or make generalizations, but introduces the reader to stories of global sojourners who have made the treacherous journey through refugee camps, across borders of all kinds, to come to America on the promise that America is a place of opportunity, welcome, and hope for a future, for the transformative power of connecting with people, and for the power of relationships which transcend borders of all kinds. The discussion questions at the conclusion of each chapter provide a way for the reader to engage in lively conversation with a book club, faith group, or anyone wanting to engage in ways to build bridges and welcome the stranger. Anyone curious to learn more about the complex stories of global sojourners displaced by war, violence, political unrest, poverty, or climate change will be drawn into Rouse's heart-wrenching and hope-filled stories of these remarkable sojourners. These stories may also provide the reader with a glimpse of hope for the challenges in one's own life."

— *Robin Steinke, President, Luther Seminary*

"Once again, Rick Rouse helps the church think about how to respond to a pressing contemporary area of ministry. In this book, Rick not only reflects in theologically responsible, practical ways upon how we can better welcome the stranger and sojourner, the refugee, the immigrant, and the asylum seeker, but also enables them to tell their stories, speaking for themselves, giving us unique insights that can change how we minister to and with them."

— *Will Willimon, Professor of the Practice of Christian Ministry, Duke Divinity School; United Methodist bishop, retired; author of* Accidental Preacher: A Memoir

PERMISSIONS

1. Bible quotations, unless otherwise noted, are from the *New Revised Standard Version Bible,* copyright 1989, Division of Christian Education of the National Council of the Churches of Christ in the United States of America. Used by permission. All rights reserved.

2. Bjorlin, Davd. "Build a Longer Table." Chicago: GIA Publications, 2018. Lyrics reprinted with permission of GIA Publications Inc.

3. "America's Border Crisis in Ten Charts." *The Economist,* January 2024. Chart 9: "Illegal Immigrants" reproduced by permission of Economist Group Limited.

4. Evangelical Lutheran Church in America. "A Sanctuary Church." 2019. Reproduced with permission of Rev. Keith Fry, executive for Office of the Secretary Administration, ELCA.

5. Evangelical Church in America. "Repudiation of the Doctrine of Discovery." 2016. Reproduced with permission of Rev. Keith Fry, executive for Office of the Secretary Administration, ELCA.

6. Christian Church (Disciples of Christ). "Repudiation of the Doctrine of Discovery." 2017. Reproduced with permission of Rev. Alan Dicken, director of immigration services, Week of Compassion, Disciples of Christ.

7. "Are Immigrants a Threat? Most Americans Don't Think So, But Those Receptive to the 'Threat' Narrative Are Predictably More Anti-Immigrant," Public Religious Research Institute. January 2023. Reproduced by permission from Robert P. Jones, Public Religious Research Institute. Permission includes all graphs from PRRI included in the body of the text.

8. Brookings Research: Permission granted to reprint any graphs and references with proper citation.

9. Pew Research Center. Permission granted to reprint any graphs and references with proper citation.

Print: 9780827201323

EPUB: 9780827201262

EPDF: 9780827201279

ChalicePress.com

Printed in the United States of America

Dedicated to the countless Americans
who have reached out with love and compassion
to welcome the stranger and sojourner—
the refugee, the immigrant, the asylum seeker.

What Jesus *never* said:

"Feed the hungry only if they have papers."

"Clothe the naked only if they're from your country."

"Welcome the stranger only if there's zero risk."

"Help the poor only if it's convenient."

"Love your neighbor only if they look like you."

—James Martin, SJ

Contents

Foreword

The old lady mussed my WASP-y blond hair and chuckled, "You're good stock, Ricky." I must have been five years old, and this is my earliest memory of my great-grandmother, who (like Rick Rouse's great-grandparents) "came over on the boat" from Norway.

Filled with hope, our ancestors sailed under the welcoming torch of the Statue of Liberty, enjoyed the generous reception offered to white, Protestant Europeans, and set out to work hard and prosper. And work hard and prosper they did, thanks to the immigration laws of the day that deemed them "good stock." Of course, if you were a "Chinaman" from Asia or a "wetback" from south of the border, your welcome included the "work hard" part ... but not the "prosper."

As a privileged white, male, and Christian citizen of the U.S., I'm needy only in the area of understanding the reality of immigrants and refugees in today's world and how that intersects with the political reality of today's America. I'm a travel writer and a tour guide—and because I know we learn more about our country by leaving it and looking at it from a distance, I'm a workaholic on a mission: to equip and inspire Americans to venture beyond Orlando.

While my Norwegian family fled a hard reality for a land of hope and promise, the "old country" is where I've long found inspiration. I'll never forget the moment, on my first schoolboy trip to Europe, that both blessed and burdened me with an important perspective. My parents and I were in Oslo's lush and green Frogner Park. Amidst a wonderland of concrete Vigeland statues of generic—and naked—people living and loving together, we were surrounded by local families. I remember thinking about how my parents were crazy in love with me—then looking out on that vast park, speckled with other parents loving their children just as much as mine loved me. Even as a goofball teeny-bopper, it occurred to me, "Wow, this world is filled with billions of equally lovable children of God." That realization—that we are all children of the same heavenly Father, all of us brothers and sisters, and by sojourning we get to know the family—has been a prized souvenir of my travels ever since.

On my most recent visit to Oslo, more than fifty years after that first perspective-broadening trip, I sat on a new public bench, called the "Peace Bench," in front of the harborside Nobel Peace Center. Curving up in the shape of a smile, it's designed so that anyone sitting on it will slide together. Etched in the pavement in front of that bench is a quote from Nelson Mandela: "The best weapon is to sit down and talk."

When we sit down and talk, the road can be church. And with this book, the road comes to us, thanks to Rick Rouse's insightful interviews that help us understand the hopes and dreams of immigrants and refugees in our midst.

Today, our country is more fearful than ever in my memory, and so much of that fear is a function of being divided. Walls—whether metaphorical (like the barriers of ethnocentricity and fear that divide Americans) or physical—are a big part of the problem. For example, I believe a major challenge in the Holy Land, where a wall was erected to protect one tribe from the other, is a lack of connection. Ironically, rather than making people safer, I fear that, in the long term, walls make everyone less safe, as they keep the younger generations saddled with their parents' baggage and unable to talk to each other.

Every wall—again, whether metaphorical or physical—comes with two stories, and we can't understand that wall without understanding both narratives. Actually hearing the voices on the other side of the wall requires initiative and a willingness to get out of our comfort zone. You may feel a little culture shock when you meet the people in this book, but that's a good thing. Culture shock is the growing pains of a broadening perspective. A good tour guide will curate the travelers' culture shock ... and that's also what Rick Rouse provides.

A traveler knows that for true peace we need not walls but bridges, and we build bridges by connecting. Like travel, this book will give you a bridge—a connection: the experience of getting to know the stranger in our midst.

We can embrace our world as tourists (the road as playground), travelers (the road as school), or pilgrims (the road as church). Personally, I like a mix of all three. Any of us can be pilgrims by seeking a transformational experience that gets us out of our comfort zone, giving us that most valuable souvenir: a broader perspective. And as thoughtful Christian travelers, we can bring home a better understanding of how we are all children of the same loving God and how suffering across the sea is as real as suffering across the street.

We can also gain an empathy for the people who travel not by choice but as refugees, immigrants, and asylum seekers—people who are forced to leave their homes as the result of climate disasters, persecution, violence, economics, or human rights violations; people who have no choice but to travel in search of safety and survival ... and in hope of a better life.

Whether religious or not, travelers can learn from the books of the great monotheistic faiths—stories of refugees and nomads, of pilgrims and travelers. The Quran and the Torah encourage believers to show kindness to "the neighbor who is a stranger," and so does the Bible. In the book of Hebrews, you'll read: "Let mutual love continue. Do not neglect to show hospitality to strangers, for by doing that some have entertained angels without knowing it" (Hebrews 13:1–2). And of course (as we read in Matthew 25:35), Jesus said, "For I was hungry and you gave me food, I was thirsty and you gave me something to drink, I was a stranger and you welcomed me."

With this book, we meet strangers who have come to this country—many escaping unimaginable conditions—because the United States is seen as a place of hope. Despite the obstacles they face, these immigrants and their families found their way here to create a better life. These pages tell their stories—stories of faith and resilience—that reflect the true spirit of those new to our shores.

As climate change ramps up, untold millions will be forced to abandon their newly uninhabitable homelands in search of a refuge. The mightiest walls on the planet cannot change the fact that refugees will be a big part of our human story. With this book, we, in a sense, travel into the world of these refugees and immigrants. With their stories, like my first eureka in that Oslo park, we'll see them as part of the family: brothers and sisters, children of the same loving and heavenly Father. The stories you're about to read—the stories of their faith, hope, and love—will help us get to know the family.

—Rick Steves

Acknowledgments

There are many people who made this publication possible. Among those to whom I am indebted are:

- Rick Steves, who wrote the Foreword. Rick is not only a travel guru but also a man of deep faith who is committed to social justice.
- Brad Lyons, my publisher, who offered invaluable guidance and support of this project.
- Ralie Deffenbaugh, Beth Lewis, and Paul Ingram, who read the initial drafts of the manuscript and offered valuable feedback.
- Alan Dicken, associate director for immigration and refuge response for the Christian Church (Disciples of Christ), who was an invaluable resource and who also reviewed the material for the book.
- Courtney Richards, communications and development manager for Week of Compassion (Disciples of Christ), who provided connections, material, and support.
- The dedicated staff of Global Refuge (Lutheran Immigration and Refuge Service) for their partnership in this venture. Beth Nelson Chase lined up interviews with some of her immigration colleagues as well as refugees who shared their amazing stories with me. Eric Shafer offered initial encouragement to include Global Refuge as partner in this project. Tala AlRaheb provided key insights and a global perspective regarding the immigration crisis. Current and past leaders of Global Refuge offered their insights on the important ministry and challenges of immigration and deserve my thanks: Krish Vignarajah,

president and CEO; Linda Hartke, past president and CEO; and Ralston (Ralie) Deffenbaugh, past president and CEO.

- Darrel Jodock, retired professor and author, who provided sage wisdom and guidance.
- J. Mateo and Annette Chavez, who minister to asylum seekers at the border of the U.S. and Mexico, who offered insights into the plight and difficult journey of refugees.
- Robert Jones, president of Public Religion Research Institute, who gave permission to reprint PRRI's research graphs and commentary.
- My heartfelt gratitude to those who were willing to share their journey to America: Nassir Ahmad, Emillie Binja, Wilmot and Maddie Collins, Varinia Espinosa, Vatalii Kotok, the Andres Martinez family, Jamal Rahman, and Juan Villegas and Yuni Oyarzabal.
- Finally, I am thankful to all who read the manuscript draft and provided an endorsement, whose names are found at the front of this book.

Introduction

Just as man cannot live without dreams,
he cannot live without hope.
If dreams reflect the past, hope summons the future.
—Elie Wiesel

It is December, and a church reader board reminds me "Mary and Joseph were refugees." I write this on the first Sunday of Advent, when many Christians are lighting the candle of hope on their Advent wreath as they prepare to celebrate the birth of Jesus. For the other Abrahamic faiths of Judaism and Islam, December is likewise a time of celebrating in a spirit of hope. Jews celebrate the festival of lights called *Hanukkah*, and Muslims celebrate the prophet Muhammad's birthday, known as *Mawlid al-Nabi*.

Hope is a Powerful Image

In writing that "we also boast in our sufferings, knowing that suffering produces endurance, and endurance produces character, and character produces hope, and hope does not disappoint us" (Romans 5:3–5), Paul reminds us that hope is not only necessary but is ultimately what enables individuals to overcome adversity, such as facing a difficult illness, dealing with tragedy and loss in one's life, coping with hardship, or being forced to flee one's homeland. In his book *Man's Search for Meaning*, Viktor Frankl observed that hope was a common characteristic of Holocaust survivors. Hope and a sense of purpose enabled them to hang on, survive, and overcome.

Hope is both a fragile and a powerful thing—fragile because it can easily be crushed by individuals or circumstances, powerful because it enables us to overcome adversity and to achieve our dreams. In his first book, *The Audacity of Hope*, President Barack Obama laid out his vision of a hopeful future for America. My book is about how strangers have come to this country, many fleeing unimaginable conditions, precisely because the United States has always been portrayed as a place of hope. Despite the many obstacles, immigrants and their families have found their way to create a better life here. Their stories of faith and resilience contained in these pages reflect the true spirit of those new to our shores.

Human Rights and Immigration are Key Themes

December 2023 marked the seventy-fifth anniversary of the United Nations Declaration on Human Rights. At just three years old, the UN formed a Human Rights Commission, and it chose Eleanor Roosevelt, then a U.S. delegate to the UN, as its chair. At its first meeting, UN Assistant Secretary General Henri Laugier told the commission that the people of the world were placing their hope and confidence in them to guarantee that the rights and essential dignity of each person would be respected. The final document began with a preamble explaining why a UN Declaration on Human Rights was necessary: that the "recognition of the inherent dignity and of the equal and inalienable rights of all members of the human family is the foundation of freedom, justice and peace in the world," and that "the advent of a world in which human beings shall enjoy freedom of speech and belief and freedom from fear and want has been proclaimed as the highest aspiration of the common people, human rights should be protected by the rule of law." Thirty-eight articles followed establishing that all "human beings are born free and equal in dignity and rights ... without distinction of any kind, such as race, colour, sex, language, religion, political or other opinion, national or social origin, property, birth or other status." Among those rights were the right to travel both freely within a country and outside of it; the right to a standard of living adequate for one's health and well-being, including food, clothing, housing, medical care and necessary services; and the list goes on. This declaration—intended to give hope to millions of displaced people—laid the groundwork for the formation of the United Nations High Commissioner for Refugees two years later in 1950.

The refugee crisis and the climate crisis are perhaps the two greatest challenges facing humanity today, the latter resulting in climate migrants. According to the UN High Commissioner for Refugees, by the end of 2022, 108.4 million people had been forcibly displaced worldwide because of climate, persecution, conflict, violence, or human rights violations. This includes what is now a record number of 35.3 million refugees who have been forced to flee their country of origin. To make matters worse, national anti-immigration policies are fueled by racism as fewer and fewer refugees find a safe haven.

Unfortunately, the refugee/immigration problem has been politicized in the U.S. almost from our inception as a nation. Rather than politicize it, this book attempts to humanize the issue while also acknowledging the checkered history of U.S. immigration policies and practices. It is intended to be a hopeful, yet frank, account of the history of how America has welcomed newcomers to this country from the beginning of our republic to the present day.

These are challenging and difficult times for our nation and our world. As a result of the war in Ukraine, an estimated 5.1 million people have been driven from their homes. And because of the fighting in the Middle East, 2 million people in Gaza—nearly 90 percent of the population—are estimated to have been internally displaced, with over a million sheltering in 156 UN emergency facilities. At the same time, American politics is so polarized that the government appears deadlocked or unable to act on meaningful solutions to either domestic or foreign problems.

We are at a tipping point that calls for an open and honest discussion of our "immigration problem," and to that end I have four objectives in mind for this book:

1. To acknowledge that while a high aspiration of the soul of America is to consider this nation a place of welcome and refuge for all, our history often tells a different story.

2. To offer a counter narrative to the one promoted by some politicians and hate groups that many refugees are criminals, rapists, murderers, or freeloaders, and to debunk ideas such as the Great Replacement Conspiracy theory used stir up fear among white Americans that immigrants of color will displace them and their positions of power and privilege.

3. To explore how we can share the space on this planet with the understanding that it is a matter of human dignity for all people to have a safe place to call home.
4. To show how faith and hope have played an important part in the immigrant journey and why the United States is still a nation of promise, one made richer by its diversity.

The reader will find rich resources in the chapters of this book. In addition, the appendices offer a treasure trove for those who wish to dive deeper into immigration issues and attitudes, especially from a faith perspective.

The Bible identifies "faith, hope, and love" (1 Cor. 13:13) as three particularly important attributes of the human spirit. The truth of this will become evident as we explore the journeys of refugees and immigrants to the USA and get to know them through their stories of courage, faith, and hope.

—***Rick Rouse***

Part One

The Promise Of America: Immigrants Past And Present

Chapter 1

The Good, The Bad, and the Ugly: A History of American Immigration

"Give me your tired. Your poor.
Your huddled masses yearning to breathe free.
The wretched refuse of your teeming shore. Send these.
The homeless. Tempest-tost to me.
I lift my lamp beside the golden door!"
—Emma Lazarus

We are a nation of immigrants. Unless one has Native American blood, our ancestors came to this country from someplace else—whether recently or many years ago. Over the years, many of those ancestors came through Ellis Island in New York, while others may have come through Angel Island Immigration Station in the San Francisco Bay. On my father's side, it was an Englishman who came over with the Virginia Colony in 1650 to establish a tobacco plantation. All four of my mother's grandparents arrived with the wave of Scandinavian immigrants in the late 1800s.

The Statue of Liberty that was to stand in the New York Harbor inspired Emma Lazarus to write the above poem in 1883 to raise money for the construction of the statue's base. At the time, New York was teeming with immigrants from many parts of the world. Emma must have believed that America was a place of welcome or at least aspired to be a place of welcome for people from every walk of life. She intended her words to encourage the nation to open its arms and hearts to those who longed for a better life. Unfortunately, her words ring hollow today for many of our citizens who view refugees as a threat; and this has been the case throughout our history as a nation.

Immigrants or Colonial Settlers? A Nation's Racist Legacy

The United States was originally a colony of England, and at the time of its inception most of the citizens of the original thirteen states were white Anglo Protestants. While there were both Spanish and French settlements in North America at the time whose inhabitants were primarily Catholic, the U.S. from its beginning preferred to welcome people from northern Europe who were likewise white Protestants.

In her book *Not a Nation of Immigrants: Settler Colonialism, White Supremacy, and a History of Erasure and Exclusion,* historian Roxanne Dunbar-Ortiz argues that the United States was founded as a settler state and that it spent the next two hundred years at war against the Native Nations in a bid to conquer the continent, and likewise justified its enslavement of thousands of African people. It is sobering to consider that when white colonizers arrived in North America, there were around twelve million indigenous Americans of various tribal nations. By 1890, only 248,000 remained. Newspapers across the country endorsed the genocide of the native peoples. In 1866, for example, the *Chico Courant* ran an editorial that stated: "It is a mercy to the red devils (Indians) to exterminate them, and a saving of many white lives. Treaties are played out—there is one kind of treaty that is effective—cold lead."[1]

It was the Doctrine of Discovery that gave European explorers the right to stake their claim to the New World. In 1452, Pope Nicholas V issued a papal bull or order that gave those explorers permission to "invade, search out, capture, vanquish, and subdue all Saracens (Arab or Muslim) and pagans whatsoever, and other enemies of Christ where so ever placed ... and all moveable and immovable goods whatsoever held and possessed by them and to

[1] "Law, Order, and Justice for Some—Discrimination," The Oakland Museum of California, http://explore.museumca.org/goldrush/fever16-di.html

reduce their persons to perpetual slavery ... and to convert them to his and their use and profit."

In other words, the pope gave European settlers license to take ownership not only of the land, but also of the people and their possessions. It was only in March 2023—almost six hundred years later—that Pope Francis on behalf of the Catholic Church renounced the Doctrine of Discovery.

Propelled by a belief in its "manifest destiny," the borders of the new Anglo nation expanded rapidly across North America, pushing out not only the native people but the French and the Spanish as well. Citizens of those nations who chose to remain were often ostracized or not fully included in public life. Following the Mexican-American War (1846–1848), U.S. Senator John C. Calhoun of South Carolina, seeking to restrict the number of Mexicans who might receive U.S. citizenship, addressed Congress on January 4, 1848: "To incorporate Mexico would be the very first instance of incorporating an Indian race; for more than half of the Mexicans are Indians, and the other is composed chiefly of mixed tribes. I protest against such a union as that! Ours is the Government of a white race."[2] Soon the United States stretched from "sea to shining sea" as white settlers claimed the land as their own.

White Americans have viewed the world through the lens of racial identity. In his book *Christianity Corrupted, The Scandal of White Supremacy*, Dr. Jermaine Marshall recounts how the founders of America were European colonialists and so-called enlightened thinkers who equated whiteness with perfection. This initial basis for this sense of white supremacy was the result of racial classifications of the seventeenth century that considered white Europeans as culturally and racially superior.[3] Race was then a political construct, not a biological one designed to keep all other races subjected to one race through oppression. It is not surprising that this worldview would inform a nation's immigration policies

---

[2] John C. Calhoun, "A Southern Senator Opposes the 'All-Mexico' Plan," *SHEC: Resources for Teachers*, https://shec.ashp.cuny.edu/items/show/1273.

[3] François Bernier (1625–1688) is believed to have developed the first comprehensive classification of humans into distinct races, which was published in a French journal article in 1684.

then and now. When then President Donald Trump was proposing a ban on certain African and Asian countries to prevent Muslim people from immigrating to the U.S., he was asked where he would like more immigrants to come from and replied, "We should have more people from Norway."[4]

Many of us were taught that the United States was the great "melting pot" to which people from around the world came to be assimilated into American culture. This usually presupposed a superior northern European way of life that was white and Christian. Established in 1914, the English School of the Ford Motor Company of Detroit exemplified this. Upon graduating from the Ford Motor Company's Americanization program, tens of thousands of immigrant employees would literally walk into a large "melting pot" wearing their traditional ethnic attire, their teachers would stir the pot with large oars, and those immigrant employees would change into suits, grab American flags, and walk out of the pot now fully "Americanized." This kind of assimilation is known as *accommodation*. It expects the individual to set aside his or her own cultural traditions and become transformed into a person of the dominant culture. (This was the strategy used by the Indian boarding schools that attempted to remake native children into white children.) *Acculturation* is a healthier form of assimilation. It encourages individuals to adapt to their new culture while retaining important aspects of their ethnic heritage.

Former President Jimmy Carter is reported to have said: "We become not a melting p/'ot but a beautiful mosaic. Different people, different beliefs, different yearnings, different hopes, different dreams." This is the ideal of the American promise that has not always been realized.

Immigration Policies Reveal Decades of Racial Discrimination

One of the fundamental questions facing this country for the nearly two and half centuries of its existence has been:

[4] Nurith Aizenman, "Trump Wishes We Had More Immigrants From Norway. Turns Out We Once Did," NPR, January 12, 2018, https://www.npr.org/sections/goatsandsoda/2018/01/12/577673191/trump-wishes-we-had-more-immigrants-from-norway-turns-out-we-once-did.

"Who is entitled to live here?" Who among the new immigrants arriving on our shores should be allowed in? Who should we invite to participate in the privilege of U.S. citizenship? Not surprisingly, early immigration laws favored immigrants from northern and western Europe. They tended to limit the number of Catholic and Jewish immigrants from eastern and southern Europe.

Historian Erika Lee suggests that these limits were driven mainly by fear of the stranger. In the introduction to her book *America for Americans: A History of Xenophobia in the United States*, she writes:

> Americans have been wary of almost every group of foreigners that has come to the United States ... Americans have labeled immigrants as threatening because they were poor, practiced a different faith, were nonwhite. They have argued that immigrants were too numerous, were not assimilating, were taking jobs away from deserving Americans, were bringing crime and disease into the country ... Even as Americans have realized that the threats allegedly posed by immigrants were, in hindsight, unjustified, they have allowed xenophobia to become an American tradition.[5]

A form of systemic discrimination, *xenophobia* manifests itself in a fear or hatred of foreigners. Wesley Lowery, in his book *American Whitelash: A Changing Nation and the Cost of Progress,* indicates that this interpersonal prejudice

> has played out through two centuries of American history: a new group of immigrants shows up, their arrival prompts outrage and panic. Coarse, inflammatory political rhetoric—driven by derogatory racial stereotypes, which it then reinforces—is accompanied by new restrictions and limitations aimed at excluding and repressing the new population. The citizenry, convinced that these immigrants present a unique threat to their way of life, lashes out violently. This is the American Whitelash.[6]

---

[5] Erika Lee, *America for Americans: A History of Xenophobia in the United States* (New York: Basic Books, 2019), 3–4, 7.

[6] Wesley Lowery, *American Whitelash: A Changing Nation and the Cost of Progress* (New York: Mariner Books, 2023), 43.

Let's look at some examples.

Chinese immigrants began arriving in California in the 1850s during the Gold Rush. And with dreams of having a better life, thousands of Chinese again risked their lives crossing the Pacific Ocean to join in the construction of the Transcontinental Railroad from 1863 to 1869. The crews, made up of 80 to 90 percent Chinese laborers, worked in extreme and hazardous conditions. As the population of Chinese immigrants continued to rise, non-Chinese workers blamed the Chinese for taking away "their" jobs and driving down wages. Propaganda perpetuated stereotypes and promoted fear, racism, and the idea that Chinese people were incapable of assimilating into the American way of life. As anti-Chinese sentiment increased among the public, politicians deliberately fanned the rhetoric that provoked intensified violence against Chinese communities. An attack on San Francisco's Chinatown in 1877 left the neighborhood in ruins.

On this wave of populism, Congress passed the Chinese Exclusion Act of 1882, which prohibited the immigration of Chinese people to the United States. Furthermore, it prohibited Chinese immigrants already in the U.S. from becoming citizens. This led Republican Senator George Frisbie Hoar of Massachusetts to exclaim: "The Chinese Exclusion Act is nothing less than the legalization of racial discrimination. It is primarily meant to retain white superiority, especially with regards to working privileges."[7]

What about those Chinese who remained in this country? In 1886, the citizens of Seattle conducted what was known as "the great purge." The logging industry in the Northwest had stalled in 1884, putting men out of work. With a concern that foreign nationals—especially those from Asia—were competing with white settlers for jobs, newspapers began printing editorials suggesting "the Chinese must go." Spurred on by local politicians, white vigilantes threatened the Chinese community with violence and were blamed for bomb threats. A group called the Knights of Labor organized bands of unemployed white workers to spread anti-Chinese sentiment throughout the Puget Sound region. Then, on February 7, 1886, mobs of angry white men filled the Seattle

[7] Remarks on Chinese Immigration (1882), 13 Cong. Rec. 1515–22.

streets, forcing local Chinese residents to board a steamship. By month's end, nearly all the Chinese had left.

Because of the uncertainty generated over national security during World War I, the U.S. Congress enacted a widely restrictive immigration law in 1917. The 1917 Immigration Act implemented a literacy test that required immigrants over sixteen years old to demonstrate basic reading comprehension in any language. It also increased the tax paid by new immigrants upon arrival and allowed immigration officials to exercise more discretion in decisions over whom to exclude. The literacy test alone was not enough to prevent most potential immigrants from entering, so in the 1920s members of Congress sought a new way to restrict immigration. William P. Dillingham, a Republican senator from Vermont, introduced a measure to create immigration quotas, which he set at 3 percent of the total population of the foreign-born of each nationality in the United States as recorded in the 1910 census. The Immigration Act of 1924 added further restrictions on those who could enter the United States and become eligible for citizenship. The basic purpose of the Immigration Acts of 1917 and 1924 was to preserve the ideal of U.S. homogeneity.

During the height of the Depression, many Californians blamed immigrants for taking their jobs. They especially singled out Filipinos and Mexicans. Between 1931 and 1933, the state removed or pressured more than 100,000 people—many of them American citizens—to leave California and return to Mexico or the Philippines. Between 1929 and 1935, the government formally deported 82,000 Mexican people—a significant portion of the Mexican population in the state. This number would be eclipsed by the Eisenhower-era campaign "Operation Wetback" (1954–1955).

The boom in agriculture in the Southwest in the 1940s fueled the need for laborers from beyond our borders. An executive order called the Mexican Farm Labor Program established the Bracero Program in 1942. This was among a series of diplomatic accords between Mexico and the United States that permitted Mexican men to work legally in the United States on short-term labor contracts. Several thousand Mexican people moved into the "garden state" of California to help with the abundant harvest of orchards, grapes, and other produce. However, in late 1954, national concerns regarding employment for returning soldiers and uncontrolled migration across the southern border inspired the Immigration Bureau to crack down on Mexican immigrants in the United States. Even as the Bracero Program continued to recruit temporary Mexican workers, the Immigration Bureau and Border Patrol led military-style roundups and claimed to have deported over one million Mexicans. Many of the deported were actually U.S. citizens of Mexican descent.

Many people perceived the massive influx of immigrants from non-Protestant countries that began in the late 1800s as an alien invasion. Much like the rhetoric today, politicians were claiming that America was under siege. In *Faith, Nationalism and the Future of Liberal Democracy*, David Elcott writes:

> Between 1880 and 1924, some twenty-five million immigrants came to America, the majority 'papist' Catholics, Orthodox Christians, and Jews, most of whom were also not seen as white. The reaction in the 1920s was to protect the integrity of American society and a white Christian homeland by shutting down immigration and creating formal and informal restrictions that segregated housing, education, and employment beyond the Jim Crow segregation of African Americans. By 1924, almost all immigration to the United States from countries not in northwest Europe had ceased.[8]

Over the years, many Americans have been suspicious and fearful of immigrants, arguing that they were too numerous, unwilling to assimilate or learn English, wanting a handout and becoming a burden to the American taxpayer, taking jobs away from American workers, espousing dangerous political or ethical principles, and bringing disease and crime into the country. Politicians have often exploited these fears—most of them exaggerated or unfounded—resulting in the government passing discriminatory immigration laws as well as detaining, incarcerating, and expelling millions of immigrants.

---

[8] David M. Elcott, *Faith, Nationalism and the Future of Liberal Democracy* (Notre Dame, IN: University of Notre Dame Press, 2021), 81.

The Troubled Yet Promising Legacy of World War II

Americans were in an isolationist mood when Franklin Roosevelt was elected president in 1933. Americans were struggling to survive the greatest economic depression the country had ever seen. Many Americans feared that needy immigrants would take precious jobs or place added strain on an already burdened economy. With strict quotas in place, there seemed little appetite to ease restrictions even as the numbers of refugees swelled, particularly among European Jews seeking to escape the Nazi campaign to dehumanize and eventually to eradicate the Jewish population. While the state department temporarily eased immigration quotas a little to allow for about 20,000 German immigrants in 1938, more than 300,000 German people—mostly Jewish refugees—had applied for U.S. visas (entry permits). The rest were turned away. That same year an opinion poll revealed that 82 percent of Americans still opposed admitting large numbers of Jewish refugees into the United States. So, despite pleas by American human rights organizations, the U.S. State Department refused to increase the German quota any further.

In May 1939, only a few months before war began in Europe, a passenger ship called the *St. Louis* left Germany carrying nearly a thousand refugees, most of whom were Jewish. Many of these people had already qualified for, but had not yet received, American visas. They arranged for temporary Cuban tourist visas that would enable them to wait outside of Germany for U.S. visas. By the time the *St. Louis* reached Havana, however, the Cuban government had changed its visa regulations. It refused to allow most of the refugees to land.

The *St. Louis* was forced to leave Cuban waters and sailed up the Florida coast. American Jewish organizations pressured the State Department to allow the ship to land; but without special legislation by Congress or an executive order by the president, the government would not allow the refugees onto American soil. The *St. Louis* returned to Europe, and several nations there did grant asylum to the refugees. But when Hitler's troops marched through Europe, most of the ship's ill-fated passengers were caught by the Nazis and sent to concentration camps.

Following America's entry into the war in 1942, government officials feared that enemy spies and saboteurs might enter the country in the guise of refugees, so immigration declined even further. At the same time, the American public became aware of the enormity of the Nazi atrocities, and people began to demand that the United States do something to rescue the remaining Jewish people of Europe. President Roosevelt signed an executive order creating a War Refugee Board, giving it the authority "to take all measures within its policy to rescue victims of the enemy oppression in imminent danger of death." The War Refugee Board immediately began to mobilize rescue activities in Europe, issuing war crimes warnings and sending food parcels. It launched many dramatic rescue operations and is credited with saving over 200,000 Jewish people in the final months of the war.

One of the positive outcomes of World War II was the creation of numerous humanitarian groups that rose to the challenge of assisting thousands of refugees who had been displaced during the war. They filled a void in a world where there was no United Nations or international refugee law. One such group was the International Rescue Committee, founded in 1933, whose goal was to assist all those of whatever race or opinion who are refugees suffering within Germany under the Nazi regime. At the end of the war, President Harry S. Truman issued the Corporate Affidavit Program of 1946 to speed up the admission of thousands of people displaced by the war. This meant that the U.S. federal government would provide financial support to voluntary agencies to aid in resettlement efforts of those seeking to make their home in the United States. Under the Displaced Persons Act of 1948, responsibility for resettling displaced persons was assigned to voluntary agencies and state commissions. Some of these were newly formed faith-based organizations and included Lutheran Immigration and Refugee Services (1939), World Relief (1944), and Church World Services (1946). Another organization, the Hebrew Immigrant Aid Society, had been created in 1881 to help the large number of Russian Jewish immigrants who had left Europe to escape anti-Semitic persecution and violence. (See Appendix A for a more complete list of immigration service organizations.)

Fast forward to the Immigration and Nationality Act of 1965, which was enacted as a result of the civil rights movement. With some exceptions immediately following World War II, immigration levels had remained relatively stagnant for decades due to strict limitations on how many migrants were permitted to enter the country each year. Pulitzer Prize-winning journalist Wesley Lowery notes that the 1965 law was one of the most transformative in the nation's history, ending a system of racial preferences and opening the door to African, Asian, Latin American, and Middle Eastern immigration. He writes:

> The decades that followed these changes would see the number of immigrants as a proportion of the population increase to levels on par with those in decades between the Civil War and World War I, when Italians and Jews were arriving en masse. While immigrants accounted for just 4.8 percent of the country's population in 1970, in 2018 they made up 13.7 percent, or 44.5 million people—the highest in the nation's history ... The greatest factor in that change was an influx of Central and South American immigrants. There were fewer than one million Latino immigrants in the United States in 1960, but by 2010, that number would soar to nineteen million ... The vast majority of Latin American immigrants had come legally—through the byzantine visa process that often took years to successfully navigate—in order to fill vital agricultural and service jobs that powered the U.S. economy. Others trekked miles across rough terrain to cross the southern border illegally or overstayed their visas in order to access the jobs and safety offered here. Before long, the nation became obsessed with the ostensible threat of this "illegal" immigration.[9]

Throughout our history, it seems that most Americans were not keen to welcome foreigners who were different from themselves—Irish and Italian Catholics, people from eastern Europe, Mexicans and Chinese, and the list goes on. Over the years, white Protestant Americans viewed with suspicion—and often

9 Lowery, *American Whitelash*, 33–34.

with disdain and even fear—all of those immigrants to the United States who didn't fit the white, Anglo, Protestant mold—this in a nation ostensibly founded on the principles of *equality, liberty, and justice for all,* and a majority of whose citizens claimed to follow Judeo-Christian values. Countless passages of scripture in the Old and New Testaments are explicit about welcoming the stranger, the sojourner, and the refugee. Yet much of the American population seemed unable to connect the dots. In the following chapters we explore the role that racism and faith play in our efforts to understand the complexity of immigration, with the healing and transformation of our communities and our nation in mind.

QUESTIONS FOR REFLECTION:

1. Do you think the words composed by Emma Lazarus ever rang true?

2. Think about your own immigrant story. Who or what made it possible for you to be in America and enjoy the opportunities this country offers?

3. How did the European concept of race and whiteness set the tone for our immigration history and for who was welcome in this country?

4. In Leviticus 19:34 we read, "You shall treat the stranger who sojourns with you as the native among you, and you shall love him as yourself, for you were strangers in the land of Egypt." Reflecting on this verse and our nation's history of discrimination, how do you think this applies to how we might view or act toward today's refugee or migrant?

5. What were some key learnings or new discoveries for you in this chapter?

Chapter 2

The Changing Face of America: Threat or Promise?

"For surely I know the plans I have for you, says the Lord, plans for your welfare and not for harm, to give you a future with hope."
—Jeremiah 29:11

What does it mean to claim a future with hope? It is, I believe, something to which most of us aspire, both in our personal lives and our life together as a country. It is what we have in common with immigrants, refugees, and asylum seekers who also long for a future with hope. This is a time in our nation's history when we are facing enormous turmoil, change, and transformation. Many people are threatened by change, fearful of what the future holds. We need to find a way to live with courage and hope without falling into darkness and despair.

Peace by Chocolate is a 2021 movie about a family of Syrian refugees forced to flee their country following the bombing of the father's chocolate factory. While they manage to immigrate to Canada, they struggle to settle into small-town life. Though initially welcoming, the townspeople generally view the family with suspicion. When the father attempts to start a business making chocolate products out of their home, there is a backlash, especially from local merchants and the town council. The family perseveres, and they are able to build a chocolate factory that provides employment for many in the local community. They achieve not only their dream but also the respect, appreciation, and affection of the community. This is a true story that is being replicated in different ways across both Canada and the United States.

The Fear Factor among Christian Nationalists

A movement known as Christian nationalism is fast gaining traction in the United States. According to a survey on Christian nationalism from the Public Religion Research Institute, while 29 percent of Americans reject Christian Nationalism and 39 percent are skeptical of it, 32 percent embrace it. The survey also found that 65 percent of white evangelical Protestants are either adherents or sympathizers, and about 55 percent of Republicans are as well. Furthermore, a 2023 survey found that those who identify as Christian nationalists agree with the following statements:

- The U.S. government should declare America a Christian nation.
- U.S. laws should be based on Christian values.
- If the U.S. moves away from our Christian foundations, we will not have a country anymore.
- Being Christian is an important part of being truly American.
- God has called Christians to exercise dominion over all areas of American society.[1]

What is prompting such concern among white Christian nationalists to convince them that there is a battle underway for the soul and survival of America? There are two major factors, both of them demographic, that these folks perceive as threatening the privileged status that white Christians have enjoyed for most of our nation's history.

First is that demographic changes mean white Americans will soon no longer constitute the majority of people in this country. According to Pew research, by 2045 or earlier white Americans will be in the minority for the first time.[2] This is happening through

[1] "A Christian Nation? Understanding the Threat of Christian Nationalism to American Democracy and Culture, PRRI, February 8, 2023, https://www.prri.org/research/a-christian-nation-understanding-the-threat-of-christian-nationalism-to-american-democracy-and-culture/

[2] Kim Parker, Rich Morin, and Julian Menasce Horowitz, "View of Demographic Changes," Pew Research Center, March 21, 2019.

immigration and inter-racial marriage and conception. Right-wing talk show hosts and politicians are promoting conspiracy theories that play on people's fears about this. For example, the *Great Replacement Theory* contends that liberal elites are deliberately replacing white citizens with people of color in a variety of roles in society and not only that white people will lose their position of privilege in America, but that a "pure" white race will no longer exist.

While a majority of Americans prefer the United States to be a nation made up of people belonging to a variety of religions, Christian nationalists prefer the U.S. to be a nation made up primarily of people who follow the Christian faith. Likewise, when it comes to immigration, Christian nationalists believe that the American way of life needs to be protected from foreign influence.[3] They think that immigrants are invading our country and replacing their white European Christian cultural and ethnic values with foreign ones. So it is no surprise that 2024 presidential candidate Donald Trump suggests he would not only prioritize Christian immigrants but ban those who don't like "our religion."[4]

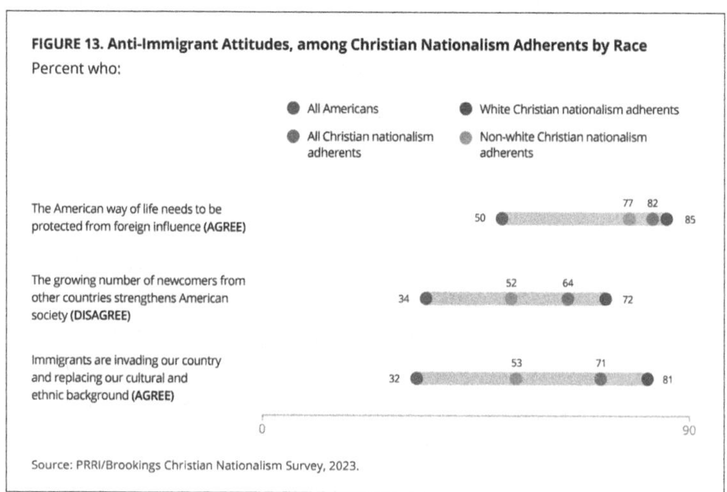

[3] For full survey results, see: https://www.prri.org/research/a-christian-nation-understanding-the-threat-of-christian-nationalism-to-american-democracy-and-culture/.

[4] Philip Bump, "Trump Pledges to Turn Away Those Who Don't Like 'Our Religion,'" *The Washington Post*, October 24, 2023, https://www.washingtonpost.com/politics/2023/10/24/trump-religion-immigration/.

The second factor that is causing such concern among Christian nationalists is the diminishing number and influence of white Christians in American life. The PRRI Census of American Religion that tracks trends in religious affiliation in the United States shows that white Christianity has been in a long decline, from 72 percent of the adult white population who identified as practicing Christians in 1990 to 42 percent in 2020 and 2021.[5] Robert P. Jones, in his book *The End of White Christian America*, writes of the decline of white Christians:

> For two thirds of the twentieth century, white mainline Protestants were the most visible face of White Christian America at the national level. But beginning in the 1970s—due to the twin forces of demographic change and religious disaffiliation—white mainline Protestants began to rapidly decline in both power and numbers.[6]

Jones then comments on recent actions by state lawmakers to legislate morality, such as restricting access to abortion and transgender care and limiting the rights and protection of LGBTQ individuals. "The need to forcefully elevate their Christian status reflects white Christian lawmakers' fear that for an increasing number of citizens the Bible and God are no longer a guiding cultural force. These efforts amount to little more than bargaining beside the deathbed of White Christian America."[7]

We are witnessing the end of an era. For four hundred years, white Christians have been the dominant force in North America. Whether we like it or not, our nation is transforming into a multicultural, multi-ethnic, multi-religious society. With the United States home to more immigrants than any other country in the world, the future of American Christianity is neither white evangelicalism nor white progressivism. Dr. Tish Harrison Warren, a scholar and Anglican priest, writes about the

---

[5] "2021 PRRI Census of American Religion, Updates and Trends: White Christian Decline Slows, Unaffiliated Growth Levels Off, PRRI, April 27, 2022, https://www.prri.org/spotlight/prri-2021-american-values-atlas-religious-affiliation-updates-and-trends-white-christian-decline-slows-unaffiliated-growth-levels-off/.

[6] Robert P. Jones, *The End of White Christian America* (New York: Simon and Schuster, 2016), 77.

[7] Jones, *The End of White Christian America*, 212.

globalization of American Christianity. She indicates the future of American Christianity is probably not one where white concerns and voices will dominate the conversation. Instead, Warren says, the future of American Christianity is likely to be a multi-ethnic community that is largely led by immigrants or the children of immigrants.[8] In a February 2024 article for CNN, author John Blake suggested that non-white evangelicals may yet save the American Church.

Why America Needs Immigrants

Many people in the United States are waking up to this new reality of a transformed society that is more colorful and diverse than in the past. Rather than fearing that those new to this country are somehow a threat to our way of life, is it possible to see the benefits of welcoming the refugee, the immigrant, the asylum seeker in our midst? Can we get past the harsh political rhetoric that these newcomers from other lands are criminals or terrorists? They are not the ones poisoning our country. Rather, it is the fearmongers among us—be they politicians, talk show hosts, religious leaders, or social media extremists. There are many reasons we should be grateful for the contributions of immigrants. The following two remind us of how much we need them.

First, while immigration has become one of the nation's most contentious issues in the current political climate, new census projections show that immigration is essential to the growth and vitality of the U.S. population going forward. Amid concerns of an aging population and lower fertility rates, immigration becomes a means for the necessary and future growth of the nation. The number of people we allow to immigrate into the country over the coming years could make a difference between the future growth and decline of America's population. Consider the four scenarios in the chart below, each starting with a 2022 population of 333 million. With zero immigration, by the year 2100 the population would dip to a mere 226 million, and with low immigration to 319 million. However, with an average immigration scenario we would

[8] Tish Harrison Warren, "The Global Transformation of Christianity is Here," *The New York Times*, March 26, 2023, https://www.nytimes.com/2023/03/26/opinion/christianity-global-demographics.html.

see a slight increase in population to 366 million, and with high immigration a rise to 435 million. According to William H. Frey of Brookings Metro research, "the population decline in the zero immigration scenario is especially significant, as it shows that in the absence of any immigration, there would be a continued annual population loss every year between 2024 and 2100."[9]

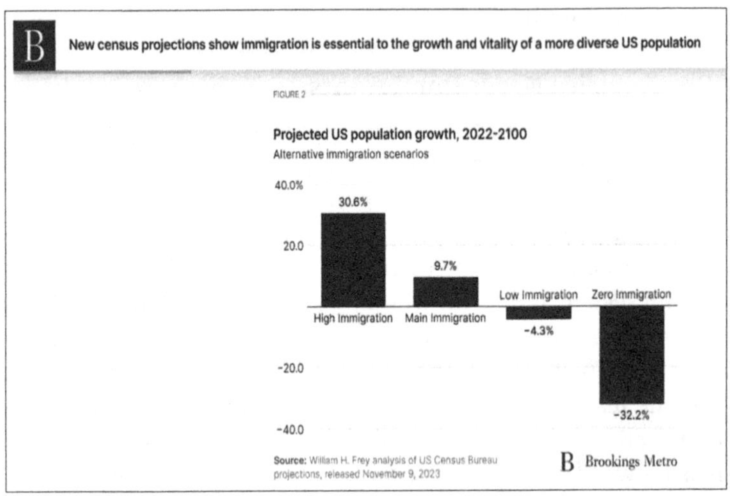

These projections indicate that, long term, immigration is a bigger contributor to the demographic growth and stability of the nation than in the past. Reflecting new data regarding a decline in the birth rate and increases in mortality, the U.S. Census Bureau predicts a slower rate of growth than previously predicted, causing the population to peak in 2024 at 333.4 million. The projection of a decline in population growth based on current trends is not something we've seen in our lifetime until now. That ours is an aging population only further exacerbates this situation. Consider the impact this will have on the economy with fewer able-bodied workers and the strain that a growth in the need for elder care will put on the entire system.

[9] William H. Frey, "New Census Projections Show Immigration Is Essential to the Growth and Vitality of a More Diverse US population," *Brookings Research*, November 29, 2023, https://www.brookings.edu/articles/new-census-projections-show-immigration-is-essential-to-the-growth-and-vitality-of-a-more-diverse-us-population/.

The good news is that the Census Bureau statistics for 2023 show that a continued uptick in immigration has resulted in a modest U.S. population growth rate as the nation rebounds from the historic low during the pandemic years of 2020–2021 with a near flatline population growth of 0.16 percent. Due largely to a demographic "cushion" of net international migration, population estimates from 2023 reveal a small gain in the nation's growth rate to 0.49 percent, up from 0.37 percent in 2022. According to Brookings researcher William H. Frey, this increase has benefited most areas of the country and may offer a glimpse into future growth trends. He suggests that these population estimates make clear that "current and most likely future national growth will depend on continued healthy levels of international migration."[10] He observes:

> Even with average immigration levels, the nation's population will experience decade-wide growth levels far below any we have sustained in our history due to reduced fertility and increases in deaths in an aging population. Because immigrants and their children on the whole are younger than the rest of the U.S. population, they will help counter the decline and slow growth of American's youth and working-age population over future decades as our senior population continues to swell ... While immigration remains a hot-button political issue that focuses on illegal immigrants and asylum seekers, it is crucial to move the discussion to a serious analysis of the importance of immigration for the nation's demographic and economic growth, and how broad policies such as comprehensive immigration reform can address our future needs.[11]

The National Chamber of Commerce indicates that the economic wellbeing of the U.S. depends on bringing more workers into this country. This is a second reason we must not dismiss the importance of immigration to the economic health and future

---

[10] William H. Frey, "Immigration Is Driving the Nation's Modest Post-Pandemic Population Growth, New Census Data Shows," *Brookings Research*, January 4, 2024, https://www.brookings.edu/articles/immigration-is-driving-the-nations-modest-post-pandemic-population-growth-new-census-data-shows/.

[11] Frey, "Immigration Is Driving ... Population Growth."

of our nation. The inflow of foreign-born workers had dropped significantly by 2020, in part for two reasons. One was the pandemic, which closed down immigration services for months. The other was the limit placed by the Trump administration on the number of individuals allowed to immigrate. While the 1965 Immigration and Nationality Act allows 675,000 permanent immigrant visas per year across various categories, in 2019 that number was slashed to allow only 30,000 refugees into the country. This was a double-whammy to the economy as the country began to return to "normal" in late 2021. By early 2022, the number of vacant jobs had surged to a historic high of twelve million, and the lack of migrant workers compounded the shortage, especially in the service industries, construction, agriculture, and health care. This was a serious labor shortage that threatened to slow the nation's recovery, and it was due largely to the low number of immigrant workers available. The encouraging news is that this is beginning to turn around. Homeland Security reports a substantial increase in people obtaining legal residence, with green cards giving them the legal permission to work.

According to the U.S. Department of Homeland Security, the number of accepted applications for foreign-born workers seeking permanent residence rose from 0.7 million in 2020 to 1.02 million in 2022. This compares with the high of 1.83 million accepted applications in 1991 under then President George H.W. Bush.[12]

The increase in the number of immigrants who have entered the workforce in 2023 is making a positive difference on the U.S. economy, according to *The Wall Street Journal*. The Journal reported in the fall of 2023:

> The U.S. economy's prospects of a soft landing are getting a boost from an unexpected source: a historic rise in immigration. The inflow of foreign-born workers, which had slowed to a trickle in the years up to and including the pandemic, is now rising briskly as the U.S. catches up on a

[12] For more information, see the USA FACTS website for graphs and a history of green card applications from 1902 to 2022: https://usafacts.org/articles/how-many-people-have-received-a-us-green-card/.

backlog of visa applications and the Biden administration accelerates work permits.[13]

The argument that refugees take jobs away from American workers is simply not true, especially now that the country is witnessing a 3.5 percent unemployment rate, the lowest in many years, and immigrants most often start at entry-level positions.

Immigration has been important in responding to the surprising pace of job growth in this country, and it is also an economic driver. It is calculated that, over the next decade, immigration will generate a $7 trillion boost to America's gross national product, according to a February 2024 report of the Congressional Budget Office.[14] We simply have to admit that the U.S. economy has relied and will always rely on a robust immigrant workforce.

The Current Immigration Challenge

An immigration crisis that is really a humanitarian crisis is now facing the world and our nation. In the past decade, the global refugee crisis has more than doubled in scope. In 2022, the UN High Commissioner on Refugees announced we had surpassed the one hundred million mark of displaced people, meaning that over 1.2 percent of the earth's population had been forced to leave their homes. That number has only increased dramatically since then and will continue to do so. What is the United States prepared to do to address this crisis, especially in light of our need for more immigrants to stabilize our economy and grow our population? Recall that current immigration law allows the U.S. to grant up to 675,000 permanent immigrant visas each year. The Biden administration capped admissions of refugees at 125,000 for 2024. However, this cap does not apply to close family members of current residents or to asylum seekers, as we'll see in the next chapter.

---

[13] Amara Omeokwe and Michelle Hackman, "Rebound in Immigration Comes to Economy's Aid," *The Wall Street Journal*, September 22, 2023.

[14] "Monthly Budget Review: February 2024," Congressional Budget Office, March 8, 2024, https://www.cbo.gov/publication/59973.

Unfortunately, immigration continues to be a divisive political issue in the U.S. According to PRRI research, seven in ten Republicans (72 percent) say newcomers are a threat, compared with a far lower percentage of independents (43 percent) and Democrats (21 percent).[15] What is it that causes people the most concern? Is it that the Census Bureau's Population Survey shows that the total foreign-born population (legal and illegal) was 49.5 million, or 15 percent of the U.S. population, as of October 2023? Is it because newcomers have averaged about two million a year since 2021? Is it because one political party in particular has chosen to make immigration a "hot button" campaign issue and presidential candidate Trump's solution is to round up what he claims are millions of illegals and put them in detention camps across the country? The latter is a chilling reminder of the Japanese detention centers during World War II.

The increased polarization around immigration is somewhat of a surprise given the history of bipartisan cooperation. For example, in 1986, with the passing of the Simpson-Mazzoli Act, President Ronald Reagan granted amnesty to more than three million immigrants living illegally in the United States. In 2001, Senators Dick Durbin, a Democrat, and Orin Hatch, a Republican, proposed a pathway to legal status for Dreamers, undocumented children who were brought illegally to this country. And in 2005, Senators Ted Kennedy, a Democrat, and John McCain, a Republican, proposed the Secure America and Orderly Immigration Act that incorporated legalization, guest worker programs, and border enforcement components.

Certainly, the record influx of foreign-born persons raises concern for some and challenges an overextended immigration system. But let us put this into perspective as well. First, the Center for Immigration Studies reminds us that the flow of immigrants was greatly decreased under the Trump administration and further impaired by the pandemic. Immigrant services provided by nonprofit agencies around the country were curtailed due to

---

[15] "Threats to American Democracy Ahead of an Unprecedented Presidential Election: Findings from the 2023 American Values Survey," PRRI, October 2023, https://www.prri.org/wp-content/uploads/2023/10/PRRI-Oct-2023-AVS.pdf.

a limited number of new arrivals; staff were laid off and funding declined. Likewise, U.S. Immigration personnel and budgets were affected negatively. There was also a huge backlog of refugees and immigrants—many who had already been granted visas—who were seeking entry to the United States. It was like the dam burst when immigration began to flow more freely in 2021—and the country was not ready to receive all the new arrivals.

Second, many civic leaders viewed this as an emergency situation, and it admittedly was that for a number of communities tasked with finding housing and providing other services. But it also became fodder for right-wing talk show hosts and conservative politicians who chose to demonize the newcomers and spread misinformation, sounding the alarm that they were a threat to our way of life. One network fraudulently claimed, "Our elected leaders have allowed our country to be invaded ... overwhelmed by millions of people who are gaming the system." Xenophobia again raised its ugly head to block America's march toward immigrant inclusion and equality.

To counter such xenophobia, let's turn our attention instead to the contributions that refugees and immigrants are making in their communities across the United States. One example involves three Somali refugees in Seattle who wanted to help fill a void for health care left by several national chain drug stores abandoning the urban core. A new and very different kind of pharmacy has emerged, run by a former Bartell pharmacist, Ahmed Ali, and his two business partners. They have opened two stores located near Seattle's light rail stations, and the model in those two stories is of a community-centered pharmacy focused on strong customer relationships with a menu of health care services.

Much like the chocolatier in the story at the beginning of this chapter, most of these foreign-born newcomers are grateful to be here and have embraced America as their own. They not only want to make a better life for themselves and their families, but they also want to contribute to the health and well-being of their newly adopted country. They are hard workers, they pay taxes, they help their neighbors in need, and they seek to be good citizens. The stories in this book are but a sampling of good people enriching lives and making their little corner of this nation a better place.

I recall a restaurant receipt that I was given following a meal in New York City not long ago. After the amount due were the words: "Immigrants make America great. They also cooked your food and served it today. Come again." I thank God for immigrants. There is no question that the immigration system in this country needs reform. There is no question that we need to move beyond the political skirmishes and focus on humanitarian solutions to immigration. In the next chapter we will explore the challenges that displaced people around the world encounter as they seek to find a new, safe place to call home.

QUESTIONS FOR REFLECTION:

1. How would you describe the worldview of a white Christian nationalist? What makes them so fearful about the influx of immigrants to this country?

2. What is the Great Replacement Theory, and why is it so dangerous?

3. This chapter suggests there are at least two good reasons the nation needs immigrants. What are they? Do you agree or disagree?

4. Many people believe that we are facing an immigration crisis. Why do you think that is?

5. How do members of the white population make generalizations about today's immigrants? How does racism and/or fear of the other affect our perceptions?

6. How might it be helpful to focus on the contributions immigrants are making in our communities and our country? Do you have any personal stories you can share?

Chapter 3

Desolation and Restoration: The Refugee's Journey

"When the gospel has become bad news to the poor,
to the oppressed,
to the broken hearted and imprisoned
and is good news to the proud,
self-righteous and privileged instead,
it is no longer the gospel of Jesus.
—Beth Moore

On a visit to the Anglican Cathedral in Melbourne, I was moved by a monument to refugees that Australian artists Ben Quilty and Mirra Whale had constructed out of orange life vests. Quilty had traveled to Greece with author Richard Flanagan at the invitation of World Vision to witness and document the Syrian refugee crisis in January 2016. They visited transit camps on the island of Lesbos and watched as asylum seekers reached the shore after a perilous voyage over open sea. Reflecting on a few days of watching desperate people come by boat, the artist said that it was the greatest human trauma he had ever seen, a profoundly graphic and devastating thing to witness. While there, he and Flanagan discovered that a great many of the orange vests were imitations of well-known brands, packed instead with grass and cheap material that can quickly become waterlogged and heavy—threatening life rather than offering safety. Quilty brought a quantity of these vests back to Australia to repurpose into a work of art titled "Not a Creature Was Stirring."

This artistic creation, located in the entryway of the Melbourne church, was made of life jackets abandoned by asylum seekers stitched together as an orange tower meant to resemble a modernistic Christmas tree. At the top of the tree was a light flashing "SOS," like a distress beacon. Quilty suggests that, at first, the Christmas tree appears to be a reassuring sight, symbolic of family, security, and sharing. In fact, the familiar icon is hollow and self-centered, intended to offer a contrast between a consumer Christmas and the reality of lives in peril and genuine suffering. He hoped that his creation would guide people back to the central message of sharing—especially with those in need, like the refugee, asylum seeker, and immigrant.

This image haunts me still as I think of the millions of displaced people in the world today—people who have been forced to leave behind their homes and often their loved ones because of fear of political or religious persecution, because of famine or natural disasters caused by climate change, because of war or simply the inability to survive and care for their families. They are leaving places of desolation, willing to risk everything in the hope of a better life. This prompts me to reflect on my own good fortune of living in what many consider the richest country in the world. As I consider how fortunate I've been in life, the admonitions of the Old Testament prophets as well as of Jesus in the gospels remind me that God calls us to care for the oppressed, the less fortunate, those on the margins. The Beatitudes revealed in the Sermon on the Mount (Mt. 5:1–12) read as Jesus' manifesto for the transformation of society. The promise of God's deliverance and blessing is for those who are afflicted and oppressed. New Testament scholar Raj Nadella writes:

> The Beatitudes are a deeply subversive text in the American context where the word 'blessed' is often associated with and hijacked by the wealthy, the healthy, and the most powerful. Jesus clarifies that it is precisely the poor, the

> sick and the meek that are entitled to the blessings of the new kingdom.[1]

So how will the afflicted and oppressed be blessed? As people of faith, God calls us to advocate on behalf of the less fortunate, such as the refugee, and do everything possible to reverse their current tenuous situation. Later in this chapter there will be examples of what God's community is doing to facilitate the reversal of fortune that Jesus has promised.

A Mounting Crisis

Massive shifts of people around the globe are happening for various reasons, and the impact is far reaching. Indeed, the political and humanitarian consequences are impossible to overstate. Migration is driven by many factors, as we've seen, but lack of food or safe drinking water caused by extreme heat is becoming a more common factor. In his book *The Heat Will Kill You First*, Jeff Goodell cites a study in *The Lancet*, a prestigious medical journal, that estimated that in 2019 a whopping 489,000 people died from extreme heat worldwide, more than all other natural disasters combined. Suggesting the climate crisis has already put people on the run, he writes:

> Increasingly unpredictable rainfall in Southeast Asia has made farming more difficult and has helped oust more than eight million people to move toward the Middle East, Europe, and North America. In the African Sahel, millions of rural people are streaming toward the coasts and the cities amid drought and widespread crop failures. The U.N. estimates that four out of five African countries don't have sustainably managed water resources and that seven hundred million people will be on the move by 2030.

Journalist Abrahm Lustgarten writes:

> In 2022, catastrophic floods in Pakistan—caused in part by the heat-driven melt of glaciers in the Himalayas, and in part by the fact that hotter air holds more water—displaced 33 million people, which is about 15 percent of the entire

[1] Raj Nadella, "Commentary on Matthew 5:1–12," *Working Preacher*, November 1, 2020, https://www.workingpreacher.org/commentaries/revised-common-lectionary/all-saints-sunday/commentary-on-matthew-51-12.

> Pakistan population ... Should the flight away from hot climates reach the scale that current research suggests is likely, it will amount to a vast remapping of the world's population.[2]

While the world faces perhaps its biggest humanitarian crisis because of the displacement of millions of people, here in the United States our reaction is one of fear and political infighting. Rather than leading the way in seeking solutions to this critical global issue of immigration, the United States seems paralyzed by the enormity of the crisis. This has been driven in part by the number of migrants at the southern border; the Border Patrol reported in fall of 2023 that it had been encountering around 10,000 people a day there seeking to gain entrance into the United States.

Americans' views on the situation at the border differ by religion and by party affiliation. According to the Pew Research Center, a majority of white Christians (including 70 percent of white Evangelicals) say the large number of migrants at the southern border is a "crisis" for the United States. However, most black Protestants, Hispanic Catholics, and the religiously unaffiliated—people who describe themselves as atheist, agnostic, or nothing in particular and are often called "nones"—say the situation at the border is at least a major problem. The differences between religious groups on many of these questions are in line with broader divisions between Republicans and Democrats. White Christians—especially white Evangelical Protestants but also white Catholics—mostly vote for Republican candidates. By contrast, black Protestants, Hispanic Catholics and the "nones" mostly vote Democratic. And Democrats are far less likely than Republicans to view the situation as a crisis or say the migrant surge is driving up crime. (See the 2024 Pew survey below.[3])

---

[2] Jeff Goodell, *The Heat Will Kill You First: Life and Death on a Scorched Planet* (New York: Little, Brown, and Company, 2023), 89–90.

[3] Dalia Fahmy, "U.S. Christians More Likely Than 'Nones' to Say Situation at the Border Is a Crisis," Pew Research Center, March 4, 2024, https://www.pewresearch.org/short-reads/2024/03/04/us-christians-more-likely-than-nones-to-say-situation-at-the-border-is-a-crisis/#:~:text=Majorities%20of%20White%20Christian%20groups,57%25%20of%20White%20nonevangelical%20Protestants.

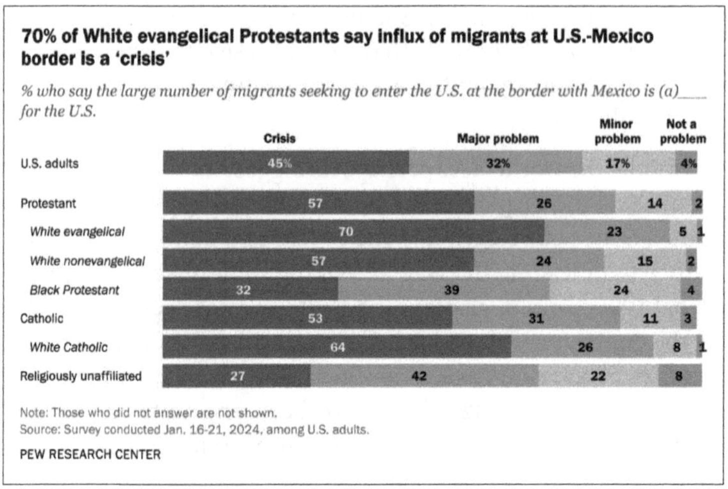

Fearing an invasion by their brown-skinned neighbors, Texas has taken extreme measures to prevent "illegals" from crossing into the state. The state has installed controversial buoys in the Rio Grande that include round blades like those on circular saws. The blades sit between large balls that spin so no one can climb over. The buoys cover about a thousand feet of the river that divides Texas from Mexico. Brian Kaylor, editor-in-chief of *Word&Way*, reported that Texas officials ordered state Department of Public Safety troopers to push migrants back into the river. "A trooper-medic shared concerns about ... a man who suffered a significant leg injury rescuing his child from a razor wire trap in the river, a woman who suffered a miscarriage after getting trapped in the wire, and a woman and her two children who drowned after trying to cross in a more dangerous part of the river free from wire traps." Kaylor concluded: "Such inhumane treatment of people fleeing violence at home and seeking greater opportunities here is a natural outgrowth of inhumane rhetoric about migrants by Texas Governor Greg Abbott and other politicians. Dehumanizing rhetoric often precedes dehumanizing actions."[4] The PRRI survey results below offer an interesting breakdown of people's responses, according to religion, politics, and what news media people watch that influence such attitudes.

[4] Brian Kaylor, "Quick Take," *Word&Way*, July 21, 2023.

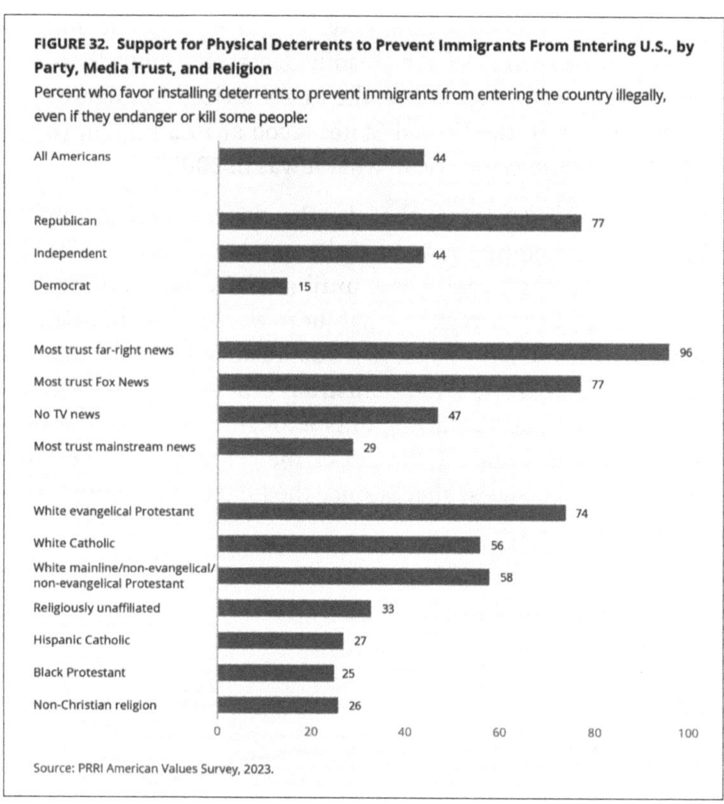

Governor Abbott of Texas also signed an order authorizing state police to arrest anyone who so much as *appeared suspicious* of being an illegal migrant. This has understandably terrorized the Hispanic population—who make up 40 percent of the state's population—and Hispanic leaders have encouraged everyone in that community to carry their U.S. passport or birth certificate in case they are stopped and questioned.

Gaining a Proper Perspective

Politicians from both sides of the aisle have given Americans the impression that we're experiencing an invasion at our borders. However, a new Pew Research Center report released in November of 2023

> not only shatters that myth but also reveals that the opposite is true. According to the report, the country's unauthorized immigrant population peaked at 12.2 million

in 2007, that is, when George W. Bush was president, and this population has been steadily decreasing since then. The Pew report found that the unauthorized immigrant population in the United States stood at 10.5 million in 2021, a 14% decrease from what it was in 2007.[5]

The Economist reports that despite the increasing number of migrants reaching the border, the number of people actually living in America illegally had, until recently, been falling. The Pew Research Center reckons that there were 10.5 million illegal immigrants in 2021, the latest year's data available. That is roughly the same as in 2017 and fewer than in any other year between 2005 and 2015. It also puts illegal migrants at roughly 3 percent of people living in America and 22 percent of the country's foreign-born population—the lowest shares since the 1990s. This is illustrated by the chart below.[6]

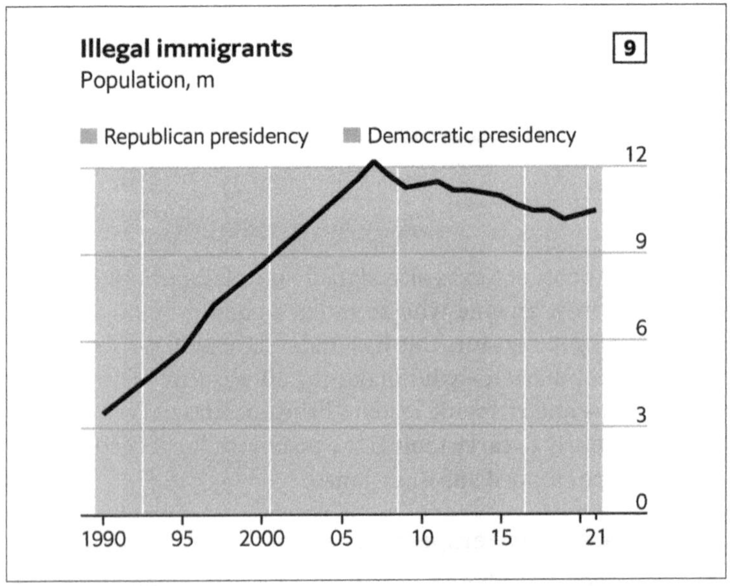

[5] Julio Ricardo Varela, "The GOP Doesn't Want You to Know the True Number of Undocumented Immigrants," MSNBC, November 16, 2023, https://www.msnbc.com/opinion/msnbc-opinion/republicans-undocumented-immigrants-report-rcna125447.

[6] "America's Border Crisis in Ten Charts," *The Economist*, January 24, 2024, https://www.economist.com/graphic-detail/2024/01/24/americas-border-crisis-summarised-in-ten-charts.

While admittedly more people are seeking asylum, there is evidence that the number of immigrants entering the U.S. legally has increased while the number of those crossing the border without authorization has actually decreased. Moreover, under the Biden administration, deportations of migrants were nearly double at 142,000 in 2023 compared with the previous year. According to U.S. Immigration and Customs Enforcement, nearly 18,000 of those deported were parents and children traveling as family units, surpassing the 14,400 removed in 2020 under the Trump administration.[7]

There may be reason for the confusion. News commentators and politicians at political rallies who are more concerned about making headlines than about sharing thoughtful analysis are bombarding voters with myriad figures and reports. *The truth of the matter is that immigration is a complex, human matter that should not be treated as another cultural wedge issue.* For example, we have the Dreamers who are undocumented immigrants who came to the United States as children, lived and attended school here, and identify as American. There are also children who were born here and so are U.S. citizens but whose parents were either undocumented or overstayed their visa and have since been deported. Elizabeth Camarillo Gutierrez writes about her traumatic experience of having to grow up in America without her parents in her 2024 book *My Side of the River*. Then we have the asylum seekers who are currently trying to enter the country at the southern border. They are coming not only from countries in Latin America, but also from China, Ukraine, Russia, and elsewhere because the normal ports of entry are either overwhelmed or otherwise not available to them. Finally, 69 percent of those granted permanent status in the U.S. qualify because of family ties to existing citizens or permanent residents.[8]

---

[7] Maria Sacchetti, "Deportations of Migrants Rise to More Than 142,000 under Biden," *Washington Post*, December 29, 2023, https://www.washingtonpost.com/immigration/2023/12/29/immigrants-ice-border-deportations-2023/.

[8] "International Migration Outlook 2023," OECD iLibrary, October 23, 2023, https://www.oecd-ilibrary.org/sites/b0f40584-en/index.html?itemId=/content/publication/b0f40584-en.

Much of the uproar over the number of border crossings in recent months is the result of two factors. The first is that most Americans don't have a clear understanding of why asylum seekers are there or that they are normally granted temporary legal status. The second is that the U.S. wasn't prepared to receive the flood of people who started arriving in late 2022, the immigration infrastructure having been almost shut down since 2019. Asylum seekers are different from other refugees. According to both international and U.S. immigration policy, they are eligible to apply for asylum in this country for a number of reasons including political and religious persecution. Individuals seeking asylum must have no criminal record and be able to show that their lives could be in danger or threatened should they return to their homeland. They have to complete a twenty-four-page document that is carefully reviewed before they can enter the country for a hearing on their status. While waiting to receive a temporary entry visa, they reside in camps on the Mexican side of the border, supported by church groups and charitable agencies, where they receive food, shelter, and legal aid. Once they are granted temporary residence, they are assigned a sponsor who is responsible for them. They receive no public assistance, are not eligible for food stamps, etc. Some wait up to ten years for a court date. They can be deported at any time.

The Biden administration has adopted an approach at the border that combines new legal pathways to enter the country with more restrictions on asylum for those who cross the border illegally. Including those legal pathways, migrants crossed the border 240,988 times in October 2023, which is down 11 percent from 269,735 the previous month.[9] In December 2023, Secretary of State Antony Blinken, Secretary of Homeland Security Alejandro Mayorkas, and White House Homeland Security Advisor Liz Sherwood-Randall met with Mexican President López Obrador to discuss border challenges, all in the spirit of the 2022 Los Angeles Declaration for Migration and Protection, an agreement between twenty-one Caribbean and Latin American nations, including the

[9] "Illegal Border Crossings into the US Drop in October after a 3-Month Streak of Increases," Associated Press, November 14, 2023, https://apnews.com/article/biden-mexico-border-crossings-asylum-immigration-def50446bc397ebfba36ab272dbc0a27.

United States, to strengthen international frameworks to make migration safe, orderly, and humane. In February 2024, CNN reported that following those talks there was a substantial decrease in daily border crossings from 11,000 in December 2023 to 4,000 by late January 2024.

The Challenges Facing Refugees

People seeking to immigrate to the United States or other countries face numerous obstacles and challenges. Many of them face a treacherous journey from their homeland to a place of refuge, whether it be crossing stormy seas or desert wastelands. They risk their lives and those of their family members in the hope of finding shelter and a chance at a better life. For those fortunate enough to make the journey safely, there is need for emergency housing, food, and heath care. Many countries around the world have chosen to host refugees in camps, adhering to UN guidelines. It is in these camps that nongovernmental organizations and host governments provide services to migrant populations. Upon arrival, each person must register as a refugee with the UN High Commissioner for Refugees. Some camps, such as Dadaab Refugee Camp in Kenya, have over 200,000 registered refugees.

Many families reside in these camps for decades waiting for a country to approve them for relocation. Only a small fraction of these refugees will ever be resettled. The process of getting accepted by a country can be long and arduous, as the following illustrates.

1. The refugee is subjected to a thorough screening process, which begins when the UN collects identifying documents and performs an initial assessment. Typically, a year later the refugee is interviewed again to confirm their status and to see if there is a need for resettlement. Only those who are deemed the most vulnerable are chosen to move forward in the screening process. They represent only 1 percent of the global refugee population. This process can take several years, and should anything in their personal life change, such as a marriage or the birth of a child, the entire process starts over.

2. The UN submits the approved candidate to the thirty-six countries that have resettlement programs. These countries then choose which refugees will be a good fit. Those individuals or families selected to come to the U.S. are put through a U.S. screening process, which is the most rigorous for anyone seeking to enter the country.
3. Additional information is compiled, and the candidate is interviewed by the National Terrorism Center, the FBI, the Department of Homeland Security, and the State Department. Fingerprints are screened against data bases of the FBI and the Department of Defense. If at any time a security issue arises, the process halts and the candidate is rejected.
4. The next step is medical screening, and the candidate can be rejected for a variety of reasons. If the medical exam is passed, authorities determine where the refugee is best placed for resettlement.
5. At this point in the process the refugee is usually sponsored by one of a number of faith-based or charitable resettlement agencies. Those refugees who make it through the process and are given permission to resettle in the U.S. are required to apply for their green card within a year and be subject to additional interviews; this enables them to seek employment. It is evident that those refugees who resettle here are vetted more than any other class of traveler to the United States.

Americans to the Rescue

So what happens when an individual or family first arrives in this country? How do they begin their new life in America? Let's look at some examples in which faith communities and others have stepped up to the joy and the challenge of helping to resettle and orient new immigrants. Two of the many nonprofit agencies assisting newcomers are Week of Compassion, the immigration ministry of the Christian Church (Disciples of Christ) denomination, and Global Refuge, also known as Lutheran

Immigration and Refugee Services. Their stories of kindness and hope follow.

Faith Communities Assist Afghan Refugees

In the fall of 2021, as Afghans evacuated and many resettled in the United States, Ashland Christian Church and First Baptist Church of Ashland, Virginia, joined forces to start a refugee response to offer welcome and hope to arriving families. Working alongside Reestablish Richmond, a local assistance agency, these churches trained volunteers, and soon First Baptist was hosting English as a second language (ESL) classes and youth art programs. Volunteers from Ashland Christian served as drivers for anyone who needed help, provided child care during classes and other programs, and served as conversation partners in class.

The outpouring of support and resources from the Ashland community led to yet another expression of hospitality. On the third Saturday of each month, more than 150 people now visit the Disciples Depot. With this continued partnership hosted by Ashland Christian Church, and volunteers joining from First Baptist and the community, families select from clothes, toys, kitchen items, even furniture and bicycles. Physician Lily Cameron, who was a child when her family emigrated from Iran in the 1980s, was thrilled to be one of the volunteers helping new refugees. Reflecting on those warmly welcomed and their eager hosts, she remarked on the power of such genuinely responsive ministry to transform the lives of all involved: "We see the impact on individuals ... It's to say you are welcome here. We want you to know you're part of our community. You are our neighbor, and we are happy you're here. 'Love your neighbor' is literal. We put our beliefs into practice."

Lutherans Help Resettle Venezuelan Family

When a family of four came to the United States from Venezuela, they weren't sure what to expect—but their anxiety was quickly quelled by the smiling faces awaiting them at the airport. Forced to flee their home country in 2016, they were finally welcomed into the United States seven years later, arriving in Florida in the fall of 2023. On arrival, the father admitted: "We are nervous because we came to a new place. We are scared to start over, but we do feel safe."

Staff from Lutheran Services of Florida then took them to their new home. Volunteers had furnished it and filled the refrigerator with familiar foods. The mother later reflected: "It was so beautiful. All this was so beautiful for us because it is the first experience of our trip. Everyone was so nice to us, and we have been treated so well."

The family had several follow-up meetings with the staff and volunteers from Lutheran Services of Florida to review what would be done to help them get settled. This included enrolling the children in school and the adults in ESL classes, arranging for doctor and dentist visits, helping them learn the public transportation system, etc. One staff member remarked: "When you see them do well, you can be satisfied. You serve somebody today, and then ten years from now you see them really successful and very happy, and you say, 'This person played a part in my growth in this country.'"

Families Foster and Adopt Migrant Children

The Forgione family first met Oleh, a young man living in a Ukrainian orphanage, in 2016 as part of an international exchange program. Over the course of four years, he visited Heidi, Mike, and their son in Texas over Christmas and during summer vacations, quickly becoming a fixture at their home. The pandemic brought an end to the visits, but the Forgiones kept in touch via Facebook and Messenger with Oleh, who had gone to live with a foster family in Ukraine.

When the war broke out, Oleh and his ten foster brothers and sisters were forced to flee to Poland—and after living there for several months, Oleh turned eighteen. Oleh's foster mom asked the Forgione family if they would be open to bringing him to the United States through Uniting for Ukraine, a new humanitarian parole program that allows groups in the U.S. to sponsor Ukrainian individuals and families. Heidi says their answer was immediate. "Of course, she said, "Oleh is family. And so we thought, if we can bring him here to America, we can at least give him a safe place to live." With the help of Lutheran Immigration and Refugee Services, the Forgione family was approved as his new foster family and Oleh was on his way back to Texas. He was back safe with people who loved him and soon adopted him as their own.

Foster families across the country are also helping move children from overwhelmed government facilities. According to the U.S. Customs and Border Protection, authorities encountered nearly 140,000 unaccompanied minors at the border with Mexico in 2023. Faith and community groups are busy recruiting more foster families to assist with the ten thousand children who still need to be placed. "It's amazing the quantity of children who are coming," said Mónica Farías, who leads the Unaccompanied Refugee Minors Program for Catholic Charities of the Archdiocese of Miami. "We're actively recruiting parents."[10]

Word&Way reports:

> Program leaders have been going to churches and other community organizations every weekend to find more families like Andy and Caroline Hazelton, foster parents of Sol, [an underage refugee]. Over the past four years, the Hazeltons—a couple in their early 30s living in a Miami suburb, with three biological daughters ages 8, 6 and almost 2—have fostered five migrant minors for several months and more for shorter periods. Two teens were from Afghanistan, but most came from Central America. "Our faith inspired us," Andy Hazelton said, adding they felt the need to respond to the Gospel exhortation of helping others as one would help Jesus when they heard about families being separated at the border. Like other foster families, the Hazeltons say they focus not on the often stridently divisive politics of immigration, but simply on assisting children in need.[11]

---

[10] Giovanna Dell'Orto, "Faith Groups Say More Families Are Needed to Care for Children Coming to the US Alone," *Word&Way*, December 21, 2023, https://wordandway.org/2023/12/21/faith-groups-say-more-foster-families-are-needed-to-care-for-the-children-coming-to-the-us-alone/.

[11] Dell'Orto, "Faith Groups."

New York Girl Scouts Welcome Migrant Youth

Girl Scout Troup 6000 gathered at a Manhattan shelter for asylum seekers to welcome a group of girls fleeing dire conditions in Latin America. As city officials debate how to handle the influx of new arrivals, these Girl Scouts are quietly supporting hundreds of the city's youngest new residents, whose ages range from kindergarten through high school. Many of the older girls have become members of the troop. They gather weekly in a room at the shelter for activities; they learn English, and some of the girls earn achievement badges. They go on field trips to places like the Statue of Liberty and learn how to navigate the transit system in a city most have just begun to call home.

Not everyone is happy about this. With anti-immigrant rhetoric on the rise, some donors believe these Girl Scouts are wading into politically controversial waters. That hasn't fazed Troop 6000, whose stated mission is to "make the world a better place." Furthermore, the troop employs bilingual social workers and a transition specialist well versed in supporting children who have experienced trauma. Otherwise, it operates much like any other Girl Scout troop, with the leadership of parents and an agreement to uphold the Girl Scouts' core beliefs.

Meridith Maskara, CEO of the Girl Scouts of Greater New York, and Giselle Burgess, senior director of Troop 6000, both say that the troop offers a glimmer of hope and consistency to migrant children who often have to pack up, move homes, and switch schools in the middle of the academic year, sometimes more than once. And the leaders say that they encourage these new Girl Scouts to continue participating in the organization even when their families relocate or leave the shelter system.[12]

Americans continue to open their hearts in welcome. These examples of kindness and generosity are happening in countless communities across this country. When we reflect on these stories, one can almost hear Jesus saying, "I was a stranger and you welcomed me."

---

[12] Sara Herschander, "Girl Scout Troop Resolved to Support Migrants Despite Backlash," *The Chronicle for Philanthropy*, March 1, 2024.

QUESTIONS FOR REFLECTION:

1. How might one apply the Beatitudes from the Sermon on the Mount to the millions of displaced people around the world?

2. What are your thoughts about climate migrants and the fact that climate change is starting to drive a great migration of humans and animals?

3. In what ways is the "border crisis" a complex situation, and what new insights have you gained about it?

4. To what extent were you aware that most refugees go through a long and arduous screening process before ever entering the United States? What did you learn from the information given here?

5. What impresses you about how volunteers are working to welcome newcomers in their communities? Can you share any examples about how you or your congregation or town has done likewise?

Part Two

In Our Own Words: Stories of Newcomers to America

Emillie Binja from the Congo

Nassir Ahmad from Afghanistan

Varinia Espinosa from Peru

Wilmot Collins from Liberia

Jamal Rahman from Bangladesh

The Kotok Family from Ukraine

The Martinez Family from Guatemala

Juan Villegas from Colombia and Yuni Oyarzabal from Cuba

Chapter 4

Out of Africa: Emillie's Story

Emillie Binja

My name is Emillie Binja. I am a young woman who was born Congolese and raised Ugandan. My uncle was a human rights activist in the Democratic Republic of Congo, and my mother (his sister) worked for him. He was investigating what he believed to be government atrocities and brought to light such things as child soldiers. He kept asking questions that you were not allowed to ask. So, when I was eight years old, the government came after him and his family, including my mother and me and my two brothers. We all escaped to Uganda in 2000, where we were housed in a refugee camp and had to register as political refugees with the United Nations.

Eventually my uncle was able to move us into a small house outside the camp. It had only two rooms. My uncle and his wife and my mother slept in the bedroom. My brothers and I and our two cousins slept on the floor in the living room. At least we were together. Then, a few months later, my uncle died unexpectedly. The hospital was unable to give us a definitive cause of death. They thought it might have been a heart attack, but my mother suspected he had been poisoned because he had been marked as an enemy of the state.

We had to carry our refugee card with us wherever we went, as we had no status in Uganda. We were now people without a country as we waited for the United Nations refugee agency to find a nation that would take us. My aunt and cousins were fortunate to be relocated to Canada in 2004. My mother and I and my two brothers had to wait until a country opened up. We had no idea where we would be sent. My mother went to interview after interview with the UN High Commissioner for Refugees staff. And day after day she would check the bulletin board to see if our names had been posted as being among the fortunate ones to have been chosen. Then she stopped going, and one day in 2015 a friend of hers saw our name and called my mother with the good news.

My mother went immediately to the UN High Commissioner for Refugees office and was informed that we had been approved for relocation to the United States. We were very excited. She then had an interview with U.S. Immigration and, after review of her status, was told that because she had given birth to another child—my brother, Joel—she would have to reapply and be re-evaluated. One of the things they wanted to know was whether the boy's father would be involved in his life. We were all feeling discouraged, having waited so long just to have our hopes dashed. We had no idea how much longer before we could finally leave.

Not quite a year later, in 2016, we were approved and could travel to the United States. Our family went through orientation, medical assessment, vaccinations, and a final interview. It was then that we would be given our travel date to the U.S. For some reason, I was given my airline ticket first, but a month before I was to leave Uganda, my flight was canceled. My mother and youngest brother (then fourteen) were given the next travel dates and were able to fly to Washington state. Lutheran Immigration and Refugee Services (LIRS) arranged for them to be temporarily housed with a family in Tacoma while searching out suitable housing for our family. Shortly after this, my oldest brother, Thierry, was given the green light and joined my mother and little brother. This left my brother, Yannick, and me still waiting in Uganda for our travel date.

It was now January 2017, and the new president (Trump) began to propose restrictions to immigration, especially from Africa and Middle East nations. Since we didn't yet have our travel dates, we were concerned that we would be unable to join our family in the U.S. St. Mark's Lutheran Church in Tacoma had agreed to sponsor our family, and they started a letter-writing campaign to their congressman asking that he try to expedite our travel. LIRS was finally able to obtain airline tickets for us, and we arrived in Tacoma only a week before travel restrictions went into place. We were greatly relieved and also grateful for a church community, a government official, and LIRS, who all cared enough to make it possible for us to be reunited with our family.

Prior to our arrival, the congregation of St. Mark's found a house, which they fully furnished for us. My brother and I were happy to join them there and thus begin our journey as immigrants in a new land. Initially, the beginning of our new life in the U.S. was hard. Maneuvering in a new culture was challenging. Despite the fact that I had graduated from university in Uganda, my degree meant nothing here. All of my school and work experience was like nothing. I had to begin all over again. Life became all about survival. My first job was at Olive Garden. Dealing with the medical system was also difficult. When my mother needed surgery, it took us a long time to figure out how to get the help she needed.

When you are adjusting to a new place, it is important to figure out how to be yourself. I began to discover who I was and what I wanted to do with my life. I was part of the hospitality team at St. Mark's on Sundays in addition to my work at Olive Garden, and I had just started a new job in dining services at the University of Puget Sound. For a while I was busy with all three jobs. I discovered that one of the biggest challenges of living here is that I had put so much pressure on myself to "catch up" to a certain standard of living, to prove that I was in fact living the American dream. I felt I needed to show that I was successful. I wanted a car and maybe a house, but these things seemed out of reach. You are only in a beginning job, working hard, and it is easy to forget to take care of yourself.

You grow up in a country where you didn't have much opportunity and find yourself in a country where one has opportunity. You want to take advantage of this, so you push yourself to the limit. Then you collapse for trying too hard. I almost committed suicide because I thought I was not good enough and was seriously depressed. I wanted to prove myself, to show that I could be successful. And no matter how hard I tried, I felt like a failure. I needed to re-evaluate my life choices. Jan, my pastor, was a calming presence in my life during this time. He would sit with me and help me explore my options, my spiritual life, and what it means to be a human being. St. Mark's also had a female pastor, Rebecca, who was a role model for me. Being in their presence centered me as they helped me with my questions, such as *"How is God calling me to be in the world?"* and not *"How much money can I make?"* but *"What is my value as a person?"*

I considered studying for a master's degree at the University of Puget Sound in order to become a social worker or a psychologist so that I could feel that I was giving back to others. Then one day I had coffee with Pastor Jan and he asked me if I had thought about going to seminary. "Are you crazy?" I responded. "I don't want to become a nun!" Then he explained that I could become a pastor. As I was discerning what to do with my life, I shared this idea with a good friend of mine. She responded, "Oh, my God, yes!" and added: "I know you want

to be able to share your faith. This would be perfect for you." My mother affirmed this, but I still wasn't sure. I needed to know what God's plan was for me.

I then went on a mission trip with our church to Mexico. I felt the call to be a pastor, but I was still fighting it. I wondered if this is what I wanted for myself and my future children. Seeing other female pastors with their children was helpful. At the same time, I had this idea that to witness one's faith to others meant talking them into believing. My experience in Mexico gave me a new perspective. We built houses, we cooked food for others, we gave witness to God's creation and work in the world. And I thought, *"God's light will shine through me despite what's going on in the world. God's love will come through."* This affirmed my call to pastoral ministry.

I decided to go to seminary to become a Lutheran pastor. I flew to Minnesota for an in-person interview, which I found overwhelming. The road ahead seemed daunting. Yet in the course of my studies, things began to fall into place. I was grateful for my professors and especially for a core group of twenty-four students who were all discerning God's call. We shared prayer together, discussed deep questions about faith, and supported each other through difficult times. This gave me permission to think about what kind of a pastor and Christian I wanted to be. In my head I had been playing myself old tapes from growing up in church where I heard that "one must aim to be a perfect human being in order to please God." Now, instead, I heard "you are beloved and called by God."

I graduated in the spring of 2022. Though I was still awaiting a call to a congregation, I was encouraged that fall to meet with my colleagues who were gathering to share their first call experiences. I had a chance to meet with Lutheran bishops from our region. One of them invited me to have a conversation with a congregation in the Portland area. They had been on the verge of calling a new pastor when he decided to drop out of the running. The call committee was trying to discern what to do next when the bishop suggested I have an informal conversation with them. As we talked, it became apparent that the Holy Spirit wanted us to continue, so I was invited to be a candidate and then called as their pastor.

What is the lesson that I have learned as a refugee? When things don't work out, God is going to do something else and it will be okay. Even when our family was separated, I believe, God made it possible for us to get together. And when my mother was hospitalized, there were people to drive us to the hospital, who brought us food for two months, a community that surrounded us with love. So I keep my heart and mind constantly open to what is possible. God blessed us with a community of faith—people who supported us financially, personally, and enabled us to become part of this new country that is now ours.

QUESTIONS FOR REFLECTION:

1. What moved you about Emillie's journey to America?

2. What is something new that you learned through her story?

3. What lessons does this story have to teach us about newcomers to America?

Chapter 5

Escape from Afghanistan: Nassir's Story

Nassir Ahmad

It was a dark day when the Taliban regained control of my country. But I am getting ahead of myself. I always believe in telling true stories to let people know what is really going on in the world. I am Nassir Ahmad, and I was born in Kandahar, Afghanistan. I was raised there and in Kabul, where I went to high school. I also attended night college and received a bachelor's degree in English. So, when the Americans arrived, I went to work as an interpreter in February of 2002.

I was not quite eighteen years old when I began my military service, so I had to stay on base at first. By the end of 2003, I was a combat interpreter deployed from Kandahar to a province in the North with the 35th Infantry. Later, I was on assignment in Zabul Province with the 503rd Airborne Infantry Regiment. Their involvement in the intense fighting there during their second deployment is depicted in the 2010 American documentary film *Restrepo*.

Working for the U.S. military made me eligible for a special immigration visa, for which I applied in 2010. I felt that my family and I were in danger and needed to leave. In fact, while waiting to hear about my application, I was ambushed outside my house. I moved my family to Kabul, where I thought they would be safe, and now had to travel back and forth to the military base in Kandahar. I found it is dangerous to serve the people of the United States, yet I was committed to helping them. I wanted to do the right thing for them and the good of our country.

To show you how broken the U.S. immigration system is, it took four years for my visa to be approved. When I met with the Immigration Commission, I was told that I needed someone to vouch for me that I was not a threat to the U.S. and that they would help support my relocation. I contacted my first sergeant, for whom I had served as an interpreter. He was eager to help and told me: "You saved my life and saved my soldiers' lives. I'll do everything possible to get you out safely." So, in May of 2014, I left my family with my mother-in-law and sisters then moved to the United States. I hoped to get settled and obtain a green card so I could work.

I landed at JFK airport in New York. My first sergeant, who was then with the North Carolina National Guard, welcomed me into his home. True to his word, he took care of me from 2014 to 2019. I had a difficult time making the transition to life in America. Life at first was hell for me. I was depressed and stressed out all the time. I had lived and worked in a war zone, and after the trauma of my past I was afraid of the dark, afraid to be alone. Not surprisingly, I was diagnosed with post-traumatic stress disorder. Living in a different culture and apart from my family, it took me a long time to acclimate.

It took me three and a half years to obtain visas for my family, and in October 2017 I flew back to Afghanistan to get them. I had to sneak back into Kabul because I feared retribution. Fortunately, we were able to leave the country without incident, and I brought my wife and kids back to North Carolina. By this time, I had been able to purchase a three-bedroom house . My first sergeant, who now calls me his adopted son from Afghanistan, helped the family settle in. He became like a grandfather to my kids.

My kids adjusted fairly easily and made friends at school. But for my wife it was a real culture shock. She struggled with the language and the isolation—especially when I was at work or the kids were in school. She had no one of our ethnic group to talk to or socialize with. I discovered that there were other Afghan former interpreters and their families living in northern Virginia. So, in 2019, we moved to the D.C. area where there was a great diversity of immigrants and refugees. My wife was then able to make friends with other Afghan women, who helped her adjust to her new life in America. When you first come to a foreign land, it makes a big difference if you can be with people of your own culture.

Today my wife and kids and I are living the American dream. We are safe; we have what we need. I thank God every day and am grateful for everything we have. I think how fortunate we were to be able to leave Afghanistan and come to the United States, where we were welcomed and supported. There are three things that I reflect on daily:

1. I am thankful to be alive.
2. I am thankful that I made it to this country that offers so much opportunity.
3. I work hard to achieve my dream.

The Qur'an tells us that whatever you wish for is never going to come to your house unless you make a move. In other words, it is up to you to make the life you want happen. I came to this country with $250 in my pocket. I spent $150 on an Uber when I first arrived here, leaving me with $100. From that humble beginning, I realize that with the help of others and hard work I have achieved so much. I have a great job, and my kids are getting the best education in the world. Unlike in Afghanistan, my girls have the same opportunities as my boys here in the U.S. I realize now that God had a plan for my life and my family. I said my prayers when I was in combat and am grateful to Allah for keeping me safe and bringing me here.

It was a dark day when the Taliban took control of Afghanistan in 2021. Those of us who were Afghan interpreters loved America, and we loved our soldiers. Many of them sacrificed their lives for us and our families. It was a very terrible feeling that everything we had worked so hard for—a free, safe, and stable Afghanistan—was gone. When I heard about a massive evacuation happening, I thought I could share my story—my immigration journey. I was sent to Texas by the International Rescue Committee, where I worked with Homeland Security to assist new Afghan refugees. In leading orientation classes, I used my experience to guide them on a path forward, even alerting them to some of the "speed bumps" they might face along the way as they established a new life in America.

In December of 2021, I was hired by the Lutheran Immigration and Refugee Service (LIRS). I came back to Virginia, where I now serve as a housing coordinator and case manager. I helped resettle over 1,700 Afghans in the Alexandria area of Virginia and served about 153 individuals (including families) by providing housing and other services. I've even been able to rescue some homeless Afghans who came here without much support.

LIRS offers a cultural orientation service as we seek to ensure a successful transition for the new refugees. Our goal is to help them become self-sufficient by helping them find employment and learn how to access public transportation. Refugees come with so many skills that they are not able to use right away. They are doctors, accountants, engineers, contract specialists, etc. Because additional training is sometimes required to practice their vocation in the U.S. or because they have no network to connect them to a chosen field, they must start with basic entry-level jobs. In 2024, LIRS embarked on a new ten-year missional goal to help refugees make connections with others in their field so they can pursue their careers in their new country. In this way, as newcomers they are able to share the expertise of their chosen profession, and they can make a greater contribution to their communities.

Recently I was asked to join the LIRS advancement staff as a philanthropic advisor, where I have the opportunity to share with donors the stories of these brave and courageous refugees. I am fortunate that I am in a position to make a difference in people's lives for good. I never dreamed that I would have such a privilege. This is what gives me hope—when I see individuals and families thriving in their new land and contributing to its well-being. Supporting refugees should not be so political. I think that all administrations—regardless of party affiliation—should welcome refugees and even increase their numbers. I want the people of the United States to know that we are grateful to be here and proud to be Americans—and that immigrants are the future of this great country.

QUESTIONS FOR REFLECTION:

1. What moved you about Nassir's journey to America?

2. What is something new that you learned from his story?

3. What lessons does this story have to teach us about newcomers to America?

Chapter 6

A Journey of Miracles: Varinia's Story

Varinia Espinosa

The nightmare of every immigrant mother is having your son kidnapped by ICE (U.S. Immigration and Customs Enforcement). Juan was just eighteen years old when he and some friends were coming home from a Friday night party in West Phoenix. Pulled over by sheriff's deputies, they found themselves swept up in the campaign of infamous Sheriff Joe to rid Maricopa County of illegal brown boys. Unfortunately, because Juan and another teenager didn't have their driver's license or other proof of citizenship with them, they were transported to an ICE detention center near the Mexico-USA border.

We received a phone call from our son, pleading for help. We were able to talk with an immigration official, who asked us to bring Juan's birth certificate and driver's license so he could be released. However, because the center was closed for the weekend, the earliest we could come would be Monday morning. We arrived on Monday with our lawyer and the requested documentation, only to find that ICE had already taken our son along with others across the border the day before.

We were desperate. We drove across the border into Nogales, Mexico, in search of our son. I was crying and imagining the worst-case scenario. Knowing he had little or no money with him, I wondered: *How will he get food, and where will he sleep? Is he even safe? How can this be happening to an American citizen?*

We looked everywhere and stopped to talk to a number of people, showing them a photo of Juan, but to no avail. We prayed earnestly that God would help us find him. Then, just as night was falling, we spotted him outside of a McDonald's, where he had been begging for food. My heart leapt with gratitude that our lost boy was found. We gathered him up and made it back across the border without incident.

My name is Varinia Espinosa, and I was born and raised in Lima, Peru. Early on I felt the call to public ministry and so entered the Christian Missionary Alliance Seminary in 1984. As I began my studies, God put it on my heart that I was to go to the United States and do ministry among the Latino community. I even asked one of my professors if I could do research on this subject and wrote a thesis titled "Latino Ministry: A Land Ready for Harvest." While I was finishing my studies, I was chosen as national secretary of the Council of Evangelical Churches and worked in the national church as secretary of the national mission committee for the Christian Missionary Alliance denomination.

My first call as a pastor was in 1989 to a large congregation in Lima. I served as the associate minister there for six years, waiting for my time to go to the United States. I prayed to God: "If this call is from you, show me by opening some doors. You put this on my heart to go to the United States to be a missionary among the Latino people. Now show me the right path." In January of 1994, I contemplated resigning my call, but my senior pastor tried to discourage me. He didn't want me to leave.

In the meantime, I was looking for scholarships that would enable me to study in the United States. By some miracle, I was offered a three-year scholarship at the Lutheran Bible Institute in California. I went to the American embassy, where I interviewed for a student visa, and they granted me one for five years. I was so happy that God was opening doors so I could take my first steps toward my vision of serving in America.

I was thirty-three years old when I arrived in Irvine, California, to start my studies. I didn't know quite what to expect. One of the things that surprised me was that it was expected that international students serve as housekeepers for the faculty. I was assigned to clean the faculty residences—every part of them, including the bathrooms. Coming from an upper middle-class family, we had maids to do this work, so I had no skills or familiarity with menial work. I cried because I felt helpless and undervalued. Then it occurred to me that God needed me to experience this. It was nothing compared to the suffering that many Latinos deal with when they come to this country. No matter what their status in life in their home country, when they come to America, many have to start at the "bottom" in the service industry.

My fortunes were looking up when I was offered a summer internship at a Latino congregation in St. Paul, Minnesota. While working with the Latino community there, I lived in the dorms at Luther Seminary. The lead pastor who was my supervisor wanted me to stay beyond the summer to continue my work there and even suggested that I consider applying to Luther Seminary. I could take classes there and at the same time carry on with my ministry. But to be able to do so, I would need to have the Lutheran Bible Institute send my transcript to the seminary.

When I returned to make my request, I was shocked that the president of the institute initially refused. He wanted me to stay in California despite this new opportunity that God was providing. The president even threatened to call the immigration authorities and tell them I was breaking the terms of my student visa. I was beginning to panic at the thought and also feared that I would miss the deadline for admission to the seminary's fall semester. Again, I prayed for a miracle. Finally, the Lutheran Bible Institute president relented and sent my transcripts to Luther Seminary.

I arrived at Luther Seminary in the fall of 1995, and the director of international students welcomed me. I began studying for my master of divinity degree and was able to do my three years of classes contiguously. Then it was time for my internship year at First Lutheran Church in Pomona, California, when I was able to exchange my student visa for a green card that enabled me to work in my chosen profession. I was ordained there into the Evangelical Lutheran Church in America on March 26, 2000. Both of these things brought me great joy.

Upon graduation and completion of my internship in 1999, the Evangelical Lutheran Church in America assigned me to go to Texas. I wasn't sure why Texas but was willing to follow what I believed to be God's leading. I was called as the associate pastor of Walnut Hill Lutheran Church in Dallas. I was single at the time, and this is where I met my husband, who was a member of the call committee. God did indeed have a plan!

I was called to begin a Latino ministry for the congregation, but I found that not everyone was in favor of it. There was even some opposition. Some were not keen on reaching out to the non-Anglo community and skeptical of any success. In the first year, the Latino ministry grew from twelve to eighty people, and within three years I had built it up to one hundred fifty Latino members. When the senior pastor realized the congregation was still divided on their support for this ministry, she decided it was time for her to leave. I then filed my mobility papers—meaning I was available for call to another ministry site.

I was soon called by the Grand Canyon Synod to plant a new Latino congregation in Phoenix, which we named Vida Nueva (New Life). Over the next ten years, my husband and I raised our sons there and built up a thriving ministry for the Latino community. We were the grateful recipients of a church campus given to us by an Anglo congregation that had closed because members had moved out of a changing neighborhood. Recognizing their inability to reach the largely Latino members of the community, the remaining members were thrilled to hand it over to the synod for a Latino ministry.

Most of the members of Vida Nueva were Hispanic and had deep roots in Roman Catholicism. We embraced the religious culture they brought with them, including celebrating first communion at about twelve years old with boys in white suits and girls in white dresses. We held fiestas and observed "Dia de Reyes" (Kings Day) on Epiphany with the traditional Mexican cake with a plastic baby Jesus baked into it. More importantly, we were a safe haven for families—both legal and illegal immigrants—who yearned for a taste of home. We not only provided spiritual care but helped with physical and legal needs as well.

In 2013, I decided to go back to school to study for hospital chaplaincy. I was especially interested in the multi-lingual program offered at M.D. Anderson in Houston. While I thought that the interview with the admissions committee had gone well, I sensed that the director of the program didn't think I would be a good fit. I was naturally disappointed since Anderson had been my first choice. I had applied and been accepted at another chaplaincy program, when to my surprise I had a phone call from M.D. Anderson inviting me to participate. In fact, the director himself wanted me to come. Another miracle. When I completed my training, I served as an associate pastor for seven years in Springfield, Virginia, and now am the pastor of pastoral care at Good Shepherd Lutheran Church in the St. Louis area. To date it seems like the perfect match.

My journey has not always been easy. I found that most of the discrimination or prejudice that I experienced came from other Latinos. While the Anglo community was supportive, betrayal came from my own community. Many of the Puerto Rican and Hispanic people were not ready to accept a Peruvian woman in leadership. I was dismissed and shamed.

What gave me hope was that God was walking with me. I saw everything as a teaching moment. There would always be something positive to learn from every challenge. I tried to learn from any suffering and disappointment, believing that God would work it out for good. I clung to the promise of scripture, which says: "All things work together for good for those who who love God, who are called according to his purpose" (Romans 8:28). I knew that if I was faithful to God's calling, God would be faithful to me.

QUESTIONS FOR REFLECTION:

1. What moved you about Varinia's journey to America?

2. What is something new that you learned from her story?

3. What lessons does this story have to teach us about newcomers to America?

Chapter 7

From Liberia to the Halls of Power: Wilmot's Story

Magdalene and Wilmot Collins

I never intended to become a politician or a celebrity, but I always sought to be open to God's calling and where I was being led to serve. My name is Wilmot Collins, and I was born and raised in Liberia. My country was founded in 1821 as part of an American effort to repatriate newly freed slaves and freeborn black people to Africa. The concept was that African people were to be returned to a place where they would have more freedom than in the United States. The capital of this new settlement was named Monrovia after then President James Monroe. Because of the U.S. heritage of our country, many American companies are now present in Liberia and the U.S. dollar is the preferred currency. My parents both worked for Firestone Tires, and we lived a middle-class lifestyle. I went to the University of Liberia, where I met my wife, Magdalene. I became a teacher for an organization called the SOS Children's Village. Founded during World War II, this worldwide organization is focused on ensuring that children and young people who are at risk or have no parental support are able to grow up with the care and support they need to become their strongest selves.

When civil war broke out in Liberia in 1989, we decided to flee to Ghana. In September 1990, we boarded a Nigerian cargo vessel after standing in line for three days with thousands of other people also trying to leave the country. My sister and her husband and baby were with us; she had baby items and food for the journey. Somehow she got separated from us and was not on the boat with us and her husband and baby as we left port. We had no food or water and had to beg other passengers to help us, especially to feed the baby. With as many as ten thousand people on board, there was no room to sleep and we ended up standing for most of the voyage. When we arrived in Ghana, I was able to connect with the SOS Children's Village there, helping in the school while my wife assisted in the clinic.

Magdalene had been an exchange student during high school in Helena, Montana. So we contacted her host family there to see if they could help us come to the United States. They petitioned the local Catholic college to enroll her as a nursing student; as a result, the college offered her a full scholarship. With a sense of hope and anticipation, we went to the U.S. embassy to apply for an I-20 student visa, only to be denied. Not to be disheartened, we waited as Bruce and Joyce (her "Montana family") and the college contacted their congressional representative to ask for assistance in expediting approval of the visa. Two weeks later the embassy invited Magdalene to come back for another interview, and this time she was approved to go and study in America. A few days before she was to depart for the United States, Magdalene had a medical exam and was told she was pregnant. I didn't want her to miss out on this opportunity and encouraged her to go anyway. She left in August of 1991 to begin her nursing studies at Carroll College in Helena.

Congress finally passed the Liberian Resettlement Act in 1992 that allowed for refugees to enter the United States if they had a family member who was a permanent U.S. resident. Since my wife was on a student visa, this did not count, but our newborn daughter was a citizen. I had to provide all kinds of documentation during the screening process to prove I was the child's father and thus eligible for relocation in America. My entry visa was finally approved in late 1994, and I joined my wife in Helena after three years of separation, meeting my now two-year-old daughter, Jaymie, for the first time.

I was fortunate to obtain my green card and went to work at the Intermountain Children's Home as a night counselor. During the day I was a janitor at a local school. I was working two jobs to support my family when someone suggested I might also consider joining the National Guard so I could also get paid for "weekend duty." I contacted the recruiter, who was more than happy to swear me in. I was thirty-one years old when I went to basic training, older than all the other recruits, but I was able to more than hold my own and received several commendations. Two weeks after graduation from Carroll College, Magdalene discovered she was pregnant with our son, Bliss. She then started work as a nurse at a local nursing home.

It was about this time, with a growing family, that we moved into a somewhat larger home in a new neighborhood. We started receiving hate mail, and our car was trashed; someone even tried to burn it. Then our house was vandalized with graffiti, the words "KKK: GO BACK TO AFRICA!" sprayed in black paint. Neighbors came and washed down the wall and helped repaint it. We were grateful for the support of friends and neighbors, realizing that for every negative action there can be positive results.

I continued to work hard, and after four years of serving in the Montana National Guard, I joined the U.S. Army Reserve. I also started coaching soccer in my free time and joined the choir of the local United Methodist Church. I was invited to become a member of the Board of Directors of the Montana Human Rights Network and the board of the Montana Immigrant Justice Alliance. I became active in social justice causes, and when the United

Nations was forming the Refugee Congress with delegates from all fifty states, I was asked to represent Montana. I became very engaged in discussions about immigration policy and met leaders from numerous agencies, including Linda Hartke, who was the president and CEO of Lutheran Immigration and Refugee Services at the time; I was invited to serve on her board.

By this time our children were in high school, and in 2011 Magdalene joined the U.S. Army Reserve as an officer and a nurse.

Fast forward to 2017. My adult son approached me and suggested it was time for me to get involved in local politics. The incumbent mayor of Helena was up for re-election, and Bliss wondered whether I might consider throwing my hat in the ring. We invited some friends to come over for dinner to discuss this possibility. Two of them were running for the positions of city commissioner and said they had been thinking of asking me to consider a run for mayor. I thought this was more than a coincidence: this was the work of the Holy Spirit.

Our friends became members of my team, and we started a campaign of knocking on doors throughout Helena to help people get to know who I was. I had a lot of homes to visit, so I tried to allocate about ten minutes at each. When I introduced myself to one lady as a candidate for mayor, she invited me in and we spent nearly an hour talking. But then she took me around to meet her neighbors and enthusiastically told them I was the "real deal." I went to every event, whether hosted by Democrats or Republicans. The Montana League of Women Voters sponsored a candidate forum, and the YWCA held another event to meet the candidates. During this time, the city of Missoula, Montana, had offered to take in refugees, and the Helena mayor was asked if he would do the same; he said no, he wouldn't accept any new refugees in his town.

By this time I had outraised the sixteen-year incumbent mayor in campaign donations, and we were feeling cautiously hopeful. The night of the election, I attended a "watch party" at a Mexican restaurant with my supporters while the mayor was next door at the swanky Montana Club with his. My son was monitoring the election returns and gave periodic reports as they came in. I was consistently in the lead throughout the night, and it looked as if I might pull off a win. I was still with my supporters when the special assistant to Montana Senator John Tester called my cell phone and asked me if I would take a call from the senator. I asked everyone to be quiet while the senator spoke to me; he congratulated me and told me he was here for whatever I needed. Not long after, a reporter from the Huffington Post called me and asked me, “How does it feel to make history?” I wasn’t sure what the reporter meant until they explained, “You are the first African-American mayor in the state of Montana!” Then all the networks started calling, and later Trevor Noah from *The Daily Show* filmed a segment introducing me to his viewers. I was told that people in Liberia were dancing in the streets at the news of my election. Eventually Mayor Jim Smith called to congratulate me and graciously offered his help with the transition of power.

I was sworn in January 2018. My platform had been a simple one: to fully fund the emergency first responders—police and firefighters—to provide opportunities for affordable housing, and to build awareness about teenage homelessness in Helena. During my first term in office, we were able to accomplish pretty much all we had set out to do. We were able to hire additional firefighters and police, we assisted in building 1,600 affordable homes, and we helped homeless kids. I had won election by 1 percent of the vote then won re-election by 36 percent. It was an affirmation that we were serving the people and doing what needed to be done.

I was invited to speak at the thirtieth anniversary of the 2019 fall of the Berlin Wall. Then the United Nations asked me to attend an international conference on immigration that was held in Switzerland. At both of these events I was humbled by the fact that leaders from around the world recognized and respected me. During this time, Magdalene had gone back to school and studied at Gonzaga University to become a nurse practitioner, graduating with a doctorate of nursing in 2020. Her Army Reserve unit was mobilized to deal with the COVID-19 pandemic. Then at the end of the 2021–2022 academic year, Carroll College reached out to her and offered her a position as associate professor of nursing. We both look back at the “whole story” of our life here in the United States with amazement and say “it’s all God”—it is God working through us!

What gives us hope?

Wilmot: What gives me hope is that I know where we've come from and I know where we've been. And when I see the negativity in the country today, my hope is in the younger generation. I know the younger generation will turn things around because I can see that. They're not looking at what the older generation is looking at—all the hatred and negative attitudes. So I get hope in that we have the younger generation to look to for a new future.

Magdalene: I think what gives me hope is that in America there are people with inherent good, who want to do good. People are listening, people are involved, people realize what is evil and they don't want that for the country. You can't sit on the sidelines anymore—you've got to get involved in order to make a change, to make things better for other people.

Wilmot: I tell other refugees that you've got to get involved. Get out of your comfort zone. When we stay in our comfort zone, we become complacent. Get out of your comfort zone, and become involved.

Magdalene: We came here, and others were there for us. But we don't stop there. There are those who face struggles like we did when we first started out. So you always want to reach out and give a helping hand to others in return.

QUESTIONS FOR REFLECTION:

1. What moved you about Wilmot's journey to America?

2. What is something new that you learned from his story?

3. What lessons does this story have to teach us about newcomers to America?

Chapter 8

How to Become an Interfaith Leader and Author: Jamal's Story

I still wonder how it all happened. I have been blessed with a rich and fulfilling life both abroad and here in America. My name is Jamal Rahman, and I am a Muslim from Bangladesh. The Qur'an encourages us to travel to gain knowledge. My parents were diplomats and knew the importance of experiencing a variety of languages and cultures. Travel promotes understanding of others and helps one move from a knowledge of the tongue to knowledge of the heart.

Iman Jamal Rahman

It was easy to convince my parents that I wanted to travel to England for my university studies. I was nineteen years old when I arrived in London in 1969, and I wasn't prepared for what I encountered there. The city seemed full of angry young men, skinheads who were upset with people of color coming into their country. They threatened us with violence if we didn't leave, suggesting we were an inferior culture that was polluting the English culture. I was in fear for my physical safety.

I decided I needed to leave and go to America. Why America? Having seen blatant discrimination in Europe, I heard from other international students who had studied in the U.S. that this attitude was not so prevalent there. American society was more open, more tolerant, they said. In fact, students from other countries were considered exotic there. At least that is what I was told at the time.

I arrived in Eugene, Oregon, to attend the University of Oregon and began my undergraduate studies. To my surprise, many of the students there were not very familiar with people from other countries and knew very little about diversity in religions and cultures. This, however, gave me the opportunity, as a student activist, to make presentations in a variety of circles. I talked about the critical need to have an appreciative understanding of other cultures and traditions. This, I explained, is an essential pathway to peace.

I later began my graduate work at the University of California in Berkeley. I decided I wanted to get a degree in Asian studies with a particular focus on politics, economics, and sociology, and how these disciplines relate to religion. It was my heartfelt aspiration to embark on a career through which I could help build a religious community and nurture spiritual development. From my experience as a world traveler, I had become interested in many faith traditions. I came to believe that all the different religions were part of the path to a shared universal truth. In the religion of Islam, I studied in the Sufi tradition, learning as much as I could about the Qur'an and other holy scriptures. When you meditate on and immerse yourself in holy writings, a transformation takes place. It is said that "once the blush of the beloved graces you, there is no going back to being a green apple." You are changed much like a caterpillar becomes a butterfly.

During my university career, I was active in student politics and attended an event in Vancouver, British Columbia. Traveling through Seattle, I decided that this is where I would eventually make my home and begin my spiritual practice. So, following grad school, I moved to Seattle and joined some friends in a business. I then decided to follow my calling and teach some classes regarding spiritual practices in the Sufi tradition, which has a twofold purpose: to evolve into the fullness of your being and to be of service to God's creation.

My first class consisted of eight people. It was the beginning of a new community of seekers. Participants brought others and our little family grew, and they came from many different faith traditions. Meeting in homes, we formed a "Circle of Love," providing food and help with rent for members who needed assistance. The New Age Christian Church in Ballard had heard of my ministry and our new interfaith community. Theirs was an aging congregation whose numbers had dramatically declined, and it came time for them to consider closing. So they decided to hand over the property to us. It became the Interfaith Community Sanctuary.

"What is the Interfaith Community Sanctuary?" you may ask. Our congregants come from many walks of life and represent a diversity of spiritual belief and practice. Our mission is threefold. *As a community*, we endeavor to live with the openness of heart and compassionate understanding that embraces all life. *As a spiritual organization*, we are collectively organized to thrive through listening, sharing, and caring for one another. *As individuals* in awe of the Divine, we support and respect one another's personal spiritual path and spiritual practices.

Following the events of September 11, 2001, there was a dramatic increase in Islamophobia nationwide, including in Seattle. Local mosques were defaced with graffiti and Muslim people were being attacked. In response to this, I joined hands with a local rabbi and a Protestant minister (a member of the United Church of Christ) to form the Three Interfaith Amigos. We sought to share a message of love and understanding. We began to do programs together, including a couple of TED Talks. People took videos of our presentations and put them on YouTube. The New York Times heard about this and did a full-page article on our efforts. We then starting writing books together with titles like *Getting to the Heart of Interfaith: The Eye-Opening Hope-Filled Friendship of a Pastor, a Rabbi, and an Iman* and *Religion Gone Astray: What We Found at the Heart of Interfaith.* Some of our books won national awards. I had never imagined myself being an award-winning author of multiple books.

I was asked to join the Camp Brotherhood board of directors, where I discovered I was the token Muslim. When I noticed that the altar in the camp chapel displayed a Bible and Torah, I inquired about adding a copy of the Qur'an. At first there was some resistance to the idea. But I was not to be deterred. It was my desire to create personal relationships among fellow board members and others. This would help overcome misunderstandings about other faith traditions, especially my own. And eventually a Qur'an was indeed placed among the other Holy Scriptures—in the spirit that "one might come to know and appreciate others who are different."

I believed it was important to adapt to a new culture that was emerging. After 9/11, people seemed to be more aware of not only our differences but also our common humanity. Before 9/11, it was all about assimilation. Refugees and migrants who were new to this country were expected to set aside their traditions and become more American. They should not only learn English and dress like an American but adopt common traditions, like backyard barbecue gatherings. After 9/11, it became more than just acknowledging our different cultures and religious beliefs: it became celebrating the variety and gifts we all bring to our life together. This was a time to encourage interfaith dialogue even more.

Bangladesh is still close to my heart. There, like in many other countries, the institution of Islam needs to change its cultural attitudes toward women. My grandparents were years ahead of their time and built a school for women. My sister, who is a medical doctor, built a clinic for women next to the school where she is now training nurses. This is important work for empowering women and enabling them to help their families. I currently assist with fundraising in the U.S. to support this important ministry.

What causes me concern is that change is difficult for many people. Change is happening very quickly, and this can cause people to be fearful. For example, some fear that Christianity is being diminished or overcome by other faith traditions. There are those who are tolerant of others who are different and able to be understanding only as long as they maintain control. But when faced with demographic changes in this country, many are afraid of losing power and privilege. They are reactive in a negative way, scapegoating those who are not like them. As someone once said, "fear is the enemy of understanding."

My hope is that people will be forced to connect with one another—that those of different ethnic and faith traditions will be able to connect through understanding and friendship. I blame religious institutions that focus only on their own survival rather than on God's mission, a mission of the healing and redemption of the whole world. Mosques, synagogues, churches—none of them has done enough to build relationships with those outside of themselves. Social relationships are extremely important if we want to transform our communities for the better. We must encourage spiritual practices like love and care for the neighbor. It is in this way that our holy scriptures truly come alive—for the true meaning of scripture is shaped and made real in personal, human relationships. I hope that I have helped make a difference in my little corner of the world.

QUESTIONS FOR REFLECTION:

1. What moved you about Jamal's journey to America?

2. What is something new that you learned from his story?

3. What lessons does this story have to teach us about newcomers to America?

Chapter 9

Religious Refugees from Ukraine: The Kotok Story

Vitalii and Liudmyla Kotok with family

This is about the journey on which our family embarked to escape the threat of war and persecution for our faith. One has to understand the history of Ukraine to appreciate our story. In many parts of the country those who are not of the Russian Orthodox faith—especially those of us who are Pentecostal Christians—cannot practice our faith openly. This also meant that we were discriminated against because of our religion, especially when it came to accessing the best education and good jobs. In addition, the whole nation was on high alert following Putin's annexation of Crimea in 2014. Many of us expected that he would not be satisfied until Russia ruled over all of Ukraine and that another invasion was imminent.

I am Vitalii Kotok, born and raised in Ukraine and of the Pentecostal faith. I was initially trained as a radio technician and later served as a maintenance worker at a nuclear plant. My wife, Liudmyla, was trained in early childhood education, though because we have a large family she has spent much of her career raising our children—all eight of them. When we came to the U.S. they ranged in age from four to twenty years old. I will introduce them later.

We came to America for a better future for our family—for educational opportunities for our children and to escape the coming war and genocide of the Ukrainian people. Fortunately, we had family in the United States and my sister was inviting us. It took two years after our application for a visa to get an interview at the U.S. embassy in Moscow; we had to travel there because, until 2018, there was no embassy in Ukraine. Our visas were tentatively approved, but we had to wait another eight months before our medical exams, which we were able to do in Kiev. Clearing the exams, we waited another four months then participated in an orientation session for refugees. About a month later, Lutheran Immigration and Refugee Services arranged for our airline tickets to the States, with the expectation that we would reimburse the organization later.

All ten of us arrived at the Seattle-Tacoma International Airport on September 27, 2018, each of us carrying only one suitcase of clothes and personal belongings. When we arrived at the baggage claim area, we saw a sight that warmed our hearts: there was a delegation from Our Savior's Lutheran Church in Everett waiting for us. Some were holding signs that said "Welcome" in Ukrainian, while others had balloons and bouquets of flowers. They helped us with our luggage and transported us to our new home. You can imagine our grateful surprise when we drove up to a four-bedroom house that was fully furnished, had enough beds for the kids (beds that were already made up!), and had a kitchen equipped with dishes and cookware as well as fully stocked with food. We could not believe it, and my wife began to cry tears of gratitude.

Our Savior's Lutheran Church had organized what LIRS called a "Circle of Welcome" that provided a team of twenty people including educators, nurses, a lawyer, and others who were there to help us negotiate the challenges of life in a new cultural setting. Members of the team took us to doctors' and dental appointments. They helped get all of our children enrolled in school and some of us in ESL classes. They assisted us with learning the local public transit system and applying for our green cards so we could begin seeking employment. In addition, the congregation had raised funds to help us with the first year of our rent and other expenses. The outpouring of their love and kindness was amazing. To show our gratitude, at their Sunday morning worship our family shared songs of faith from our tradition.

It was also important that we had not only some family here to support us but an entire Ukrainian Pentecostal community. The latter provided an important network through which we were able to access jobs, buy a car, and explore other opportunities. Most importantly, they provided us with the encouragement we needed to succeed in building a new life here.

I'd like to share how far we've come since our arrival in the fall of 2018. Fortunately, we were able to get our green cards and find employment before the pandemic. We moved into our own house and have been able to purchase several vehicles. All of our children have done well in school. Our four eldest children have married, and my wife and I now have four grandchildren. We have been incredibly blessed.

Let me introduce you to my family.

I am currently working as a finish carpenter and have my business license with a goal of soon setting up my own business.

My wife, Liudmyla, continues to manage the household and take care of the younger children who are still at home. These include our daughter Alina (19), who graduated from high school and is currently studying accounting and working at a day care; our daughter Yana (16), who is a freshman in high school; Stanislav (12), who is in middle school and plays the trumpet in the school band; and our youngest, Daniel (9), who is in fourth grade.

Vladyslav (25) completed his associate's degree from a community college and worked initially for a landscaping company. Now he owns his own trucking company and does contract hauling for Amazon. He married his wife, Julia, on April 30, 2022.

Iryna (23) also completed her associate's degree at a local community college. She had met her husband, Bohdan, in Ukraine prior to moving to the U.S. He was able to immigrate here in 2020 when they were married. They have two girls, who are two years and six months old respectively.

Yuliia (22) finished high school then worked in a bakery for a year, then went back to Ukraine to attend Bible school, where she met her husband, also called Bohdan. She returned to the U.S. and, because of the war, he went to Germany for work then immigrated to the U.S. through Mexico. They were married in December 2022 and have a boy who is about six months old.

Daryna (21) is currently attending community college and is studying to be a paralegal. She returned to Ukraine to visit family and friends where she met her husband, Ivan. Since men are unable to leave Ukraine for the U.S. because of the war, he too followed the path to Germany and immigrated to the U.S. through Mexico. They have a girl who is about six months old.

Our church family is growing. Because of the war in Ukraine, every family has taken in one or more refugees. Our congregation has now helped 500 Ukrainian people settle here. It is a way of paying it forward—to help others as we were helped so they will in turn assist other newcomers in the future. My family had a friend stay with us while he got settled and now have a cousin living with us. We want to pass on what we've learned about how to adapt to the culture and do well.

I recall some of the most challenging things when we arrived. One was learning English. Another was the fact that everything in the culture was new and different. We had to adapt to a faster pace of life and learn how to navigate according to new rules and norms. What made it possible for us to succeed was the support of the Ukrainian church community—family and friends who had been here for a while and had learned to navigate the American way of life. We were also grateful for the warm welcome and support of Our Savior's Lutheran congregation and Lutheran Community Services of the Northwest.

I am grateful that we have been able to establish a good life for ourselves in America. There are so many more opportunities here for education and work than in Ukraine—especially for our girls. And it is never too late to start something new. In Ukraine, if you don't go to college as a young adult, it is difficult to go back to school when one is older. Here, education is open to anyone regardless of age, gender, faith, or ethnic background.

Have there been any surprises about our new life in America? Of course. Here are a few:

1. Some people think that getting money here will be easy, but that isn't so; while there are more opportunities to advance financially, one has to work hard to get ahead.
2. I was surprised by the number of homeless people in the greater Seattle area.
3. In the movies, it looks like everyone is rich and well off. There are greater disparities in the social strata here with wealthy communities next to people living in poverty.
4. I do believe that in this country everyone who wants to can build a life for themselves, and that includes women as well as men.
5. Americans have a sense of freedom that is unique in the world. You are not judged for how you speak, how you dress, or where you work. Here, you are more accepted for who you are—how you present yourself and how you treat others.

   We now have much hope for the future of our children and grandchildren. We are alive and safe, our kids are all doing well, and we can practice our religion freely and without fear of discrimination. We are blessed to be living here in America.

QUESTIONS FOR REFLECTION:

1. What moved you about the Kotoks' journey to America?

2. What is something new that you learned from their story?

3. What lessons does this story have to teach us about newcomers to America?

Chapter 10

Escaping Death Squads for Life in America: The Martinez Family's Story

Andres and Ursula Martinez with family

Revolutionary bands called guerillas roamed the countryside in Guatemala terrorizing the inhabitants of towns and villages. Also known as "death squads," their mission was to eliminate anyone loyal to the government and who did not support their cause. My wife, Ursula, was a girl of fourteen when guerrillas came to her village and murdered members of her family because her grandfather was a political activist. Her father and grandfather were shot and killed; two cousins had their necks sliced open. That night, Ursula's grandmother told her and her sister to hide in another house in the village until their mother could come back for them. When their mother returned three days later, she took them to Guatemala City, the capital, where they would be safer and where she found work.

I am Andres Martinez, and I was born and raised in San Miguel a Catan, Guatemala. I was able to go to school through sixth grade then trained to be an educator. In our village in the highlands of Guatemala, only boys went to school. While I was teaching, guerillas came to our village with the intent to kill anyone who had anything good to say about the government or its soldiers. They also came to kidnap the young men of our village and conscript them for service in their cause. While I would have preferred to remain where my mother was, my brother and cousin convinced me it was too dangerous to stay in the country; so in 1981 I went to join another brother who had lived in Los Angeles for a couple of years. He had gone to work in the California tomato fields. The following year, I moved on to Florida because there was a large Mayan community there and friends there had told me that I would be able to find work without having experience. I found this to be true and worked both in the fields and later as a roofing carpenter in Boca Raton, Florida.

I returned to Guatemala in 1989 to visit my family in Guatemala City. It was there that I met a young woman called Ursula. We fell in love, but I had to return to America. A few months later, another brother of mine brought Ursula with him and his family by bus through Mexico. They arrived in Tijuana and managed to find a way to cross a river into the United States. They were met by people on the other side of the river who helped them travel on to Los Angeles. I was able to meet up with them and took Ursula back with me to Florida. Our family began to grow with the birth of our sons Frederico in 1991 and Edwin in 1993.

We met Sister Rachel Sena and Evangelist Yvette Gioannetti at Sacred Heart Catholic Church in Lake Worth, Florida, and formed an immediate bond with them. They had served as missionaries in Guatemala City, working as educators among the poorest of the poor there, people who lived near the garbage dump and lived by scavenging in it. Rachel and Yvette's lives were threatened for teaching people to read and write, so they escaped back to the USA. They were assigned to Sacred Heart Catholic Church with its large Mayan community because they understood the challenges the people in this community had been through in Guatemala.

In 1992, Sister Rachel started the Maya Ministry program and received a grant for a literacy program designed to teach Guatemalan women and their preschool children. The women were taught to read, write, and speak Spanish. Most of them who had come to America were able to communicate only in their native Mayan language, *q'anjob'al*. Knowing that I had been a teacher in Guatemala, Sister Rachel asked me if I would be interested in teaching Spanish.

In our culture, women never leave their young children. Even if they work in the fields, their infants and small children are strapped to their backs in *rebozos*. Understanding this cultural need from their time in Guatemala, Sister Rachel and Yvette had the volunteers sitting at one end of a large room at the Maya Ministry Center while I worked with the mothers at the other end of the room. This way, the moms were assured that their little ones were safe and the children could easily see their mothers. This program was a godsend for me and for these mothers and children. I taught for all twenty years of this ministry.

Our third son was born in 1999. On the day of his birth, we were not sure he would live to see the next day. He was premature and was born with a heart defect. Our infant son was in neonatal intensive care, and the doctor was not sure he would make it through the night. It was a stormy night, and Sister Rachel was there to keep vigil with us. She suggested we call a priest to baptize the baby. Father Noel, a priest who had emigrated from Ireland, performed the sacrament for our Mayan American baby while a Mexican American nun and Beth, a white woman friend, served as *comadres*, sharing the role as godmothers. There were many prayers and tears that night. Fortunately, Noel—named after our compassionate priest—survived the night, received needed medical care, and is now a healthy young man.

We raised our three boys to value education, to work hard, and to respect the law. There were gangs in our community, drug dealing, and occasional shootings. We taught them to avoid all of that, and all three of our sons graduated from Lake Worth High School. The oldest, Federico (33), also graduated with from Florida Atlantic University with a bachelor of science degree. He works as a therapist in a chiropractor's office. Edwin (31) studied economics in community college and completed his associate's degree; he is now an independent truck driver. He works day and night but enjoys the work and is his own boss. Our youngest, Noel (25), attended Bible college and is working as a junior electrician. He plans to continue his education and obtain his license as a master electrician.

In 2006 I became an American citizen, and in 2008 my wife, Ursula, received her citizenship as well. I have now retired, and Ursula currently works in a candy factory, where she hopes to keep working until she is sixty-two.

We are grateful for many things about our life in America. When we first came, people were very kind to us. Coming from war-torn Guatemala, we have been especially thankful for a safe place to live and for our liberty. We have more freedom here. You can say what you want and not get in trouble. If you like to work, there are jobs here at decent wages. You work hard to provide for your family and get ahead in life. One of our proudest accomplishments is that after many years of renting our home, we were able to purchase it and become homeowners. That was beyond our imaginations when we left Guatemala fleeing for our lives.

What gives us hope? We have raised a family and given our boys a good life—and a future with hope. With the benefit of a good education, our sons now have good jobs and can support themselves. We enjoy living here with a growing family nearby, having been blessed with two granddaughters: Aviana (1) and Camila (2). Having forged a better path for our family, we believe we have achieved the American dream.

QUESTIONS FOR REFLECTION:

1. What moved you about Andres and Ursula's journey to America?

2. What is something new your learned from their story?

3. What lessons does this story have to teach us about newcomers to America?

Chapter 11

Two Refugees Realize Their Dreams: The Story of Juan and Yuni

Yuni Oyazabal and Juan Villegas

I left Colombia to escape the gangs and the drug lords. My wife was only three when she escaped from Cuba with her family via the famous Mariel Boatlift. That was the mass emigration of Cubans who were escaping Fidel Castro's oppressive regime. They traveled from Cuba's Mariel Harbor to the United States between April and October of 1980. My name is Juan Villegas, and my wife is Yuni Oyarzaba.

I was born in Medellin, Colombia, to a middle-class family. My father was a college graduate and worked as a financial auditor for a large company. He believed in the power of education and wanted to give me a leg up, so he enrolled me in Deutsche Schule Medellin, a German high school. I became tri-lingual, being taught German from kindergarten on and English from fifth grade. From ninth through twelfth grade, my studies and social life at school were an immersion experience in the German language. While I spoke Spanish at home, I conversed with my friends and teachers only in German when at school. Following high school, I took classes in business and technology at Edfit University in Medellin. I had dreamed about going to Germany to continue my studies, so my father offered to sponsor me for six months. I gave it a shot but discovered it was too expensive to live there, so returned to Colombia. I figured God must have other plans for me.

I had first come to the United States with my parents to visit my uncle and grandparents in 1979 when I was five years old. My uncle was a U.S. citizen and working in a machine shop in the Miami area. My grandparents were living in Florida six months of the year and the other six months back in Colombia. I came again by myself when I was twelve years old to stay with my uncle, who was single, for part of the summer. While there, I saw my uncle's life and it terrified me. He stood all day working as a machinist, came home, grabbed some food, sat on the couch with a beer, and collapsed. I knew I wanted more out of life than that.

When I was nineteen years old, I was dating a young woman whose father was involved in the Colombia "white powder" drug trade. I began serving as a driver for my girlfriend's father, which concerned my parents. Looking back, I realize I was naïve to the consequences of being associated with cocaine dealers. That was not the only thing to which I was blind.

One of my girlfriend's relatives was arrested by Interpol. I had been given a stack of passports with that relative's name on it, so I destroyed them. About the same time, I discovered my girlfriend had been dating another young man. One night, when he found us together, he grabbed his gun and shot at me in a jealous rage. This was two strikes against me, and I knew that my life would be worthless if I didn't get away.

This was also the last straw for my parents. They told me that I needed to leave the country for my own safety and future welfare. So they sent me back to Miami to live with my dad's brother,

Pablo, who was married with a family. They took me in as one of their own, and I shared a room with my cousin. They were very welcoming, and I became one of the family.

I had come to the U.S. with a tourist visa but with the intention to study. I spoke with an admissions counselor at Miami Dade Community College and discovered that none of my credits from my college courses in Colombia would transfer. However, I would be able to enter as an international student if I could obtain a student visa from the State Department. With the help of an attorney and the school, I was approved as a conditional student and granted a student visa. International students were not eligible for loans and not allowed to work except on campus for low wages, so my parents sent money from Colombia to pay my tuition, which was $1,700 a semester. It was a great sacrifice for them, as this tuition was the equivalent of four months' wages for them. But again, believing in the importance of education, my parents were happy and proud to support my academic efforts.

I worked on campus as a computer tech and graduated in fall of 1997 with an associate's degree. It was that same year that I began the process of becoming a legal resident of the United States and enrolled at Florida International University to pursue my bachelor's degree. After obtaining my green card in January 1999, I started to work for Computer Coach, a technology training school. I served as the network administrator. While there, I took some courses at Florida Atlantic University, as it was closer to my work.

In 2002 I applied for a technology position at Miami Dade College. I recognized a young woman named Yuni, who was a secretary in the department to which I had come to interview. When she went to take me for my interview, I reminded her that we had met earlier when I was a student and she was working in the school library. Little did I know then that she would later become my wife.

I became a full-time employee as a computer tech at Miami Dade College in 2002. By this time, I was supporting myself and able to take only a few classes at a time; it was 2009 by the time I obtained my bachelor's degree. I then decided to continue my studies at Florida International University and began working on two master's degree programs, one in enterprise resource planning and the other in robotics. I graduated in spring of 2014. That same year I became the director of network and media services for the Hialeah Campus of Miami Dade College. I also began teaching one or two courses per term that included computer repair, engineering statics, and server maintenance. Later, Yuni would become the secretary to the campus president there.

In 2021, I transferred to the Kendall Campus of Miami Dade College to become the senior information security administrator, and in 2022 I was promoted to lead security administrator. Yuni and I married and raised two boys: my stepson, Kevin (22), and our son, Enzo (14). As I look back on my journey, I am amazed and grateful for the opportunities that I have had. America is still the land of opportunity where, if you work hard for something, you can accomplish it. I realize that it was also because of the struggles and sacrifice of my family that I was able to succeed and even surpass their expectations. My mother-in-law once told her daughter, Yuni, that had she stayed in Cuba she would likely have become a prostitute in order to feed her family. Here in America we both proudly work in academia and find our jobs to be very fulfilling.

What concerns us? We need to stop being so divided as a country because it is ruining the dream of America. When my grandfather came to this country in the 1970s, immigrants were not disrespected. He was never told not to speak his own language. No one told him to go back to his home country. He was welcomed and accepted. We need to return to the days of a kinder and more compassionate America. We need to recognize the contribution that immigrants make and have made throughout the history of this country.

What gives us hope? There is a glimmer of hope that our children—the young people of today—will work toward making this nation a better place. My wife and I see students on campus every day who are filled with empathy and who genuinely care about the welfare of others. They will hopefully be able to right the wrongs of their parents' generation and make this world a better place for all people.

QUESTIONS FOR REFLECTION:

1. What moved you about Juan and Yuni's journey to America?

2. What is something new that you learned from their story?

3. What lessons does this story have to teach us about newcomers to America?

Part Three

The American Dream: Reclaiming the Promise

Chapter 12

God's Vision for Beloved Community: Our Nation as a Tapestry of Diversity

This is our hope...
with faith, we will be able to hew out of the mountain of despair a stone of hope.
With this faith we will be able to transform the jangling discords of our nation
into a beautiful symphony of brotherhood.
—Martin Luther King Jr.

Martin Luther King Jr. knew that hope is an incredibly important attribute when trying to accomplish any goal. In his famous "I Have a Dream" speech delivered August 28, 1963, on the steps of the Lincoln Memorial in Washington, D.C., Dr. King laid out his vision for America's future:

> Now is the time to make real the promises of democracy. Now is the time to rise from the dark and desolate valley of segregation to the sunlit path of racial justice. Now is the time to lift our nation from the quick sands of racial injustice to the solid rock of brotherhood. Now is the time to make justice a reality for all of God's children ... So even though we face the difficulties of today and tomorrow, I still have a dream. It is a dream deeply rooted in the American dream. I have a dream that one day this nation will rise up

> and live out the true meaning of its creed: We hold these truths to be self-evident, that all men are created equal.[1]

Dr. King believed in the American dream, in the promise of the American experiment, in which all people—regardless of socio-economic class, ethnic background, or religious tradition—would live in freedom and have equal opportunity. When he talked about a "beloved community," he envisioned a society governed not by violence or conflict, but by love. He believed that a community of love, justice, and mutual respect could eventually be actualized. Professor Dionardo Pizana writes: "Dr. Martin Luther King, Jr. spoke often of *beloved community* as a way of transforming people and relationships and creating communities grounded in reconciliation, friendship, and human dignity. Key principles include nonviolence as powerful expressions of courage, understanding, trust and love."[2] In this chapter, we will explore how we, as a nation of immigrants, may yet fulfill our destiny as a *beloved community* for all.

Is the American Dream Still Possible?

Key Huy Quan was born in Ho Chi Minh City, Vietnam. He immigrated with his parents to the United States and became a child actor. He rose to fame playing Short Round in *Indiana Jones and the Temple of Doom* and Data in *The Goonies*. He received an Academy Award for Best Actor in a Supporting Role for the 2022 movie *Everything Everywhere All at Once*, a parody about the American immigration system. Accepting the award with tears of joy, he shared: "My journey started on a boat. I spent a year in a refugee camp. And somehow I ended up here on Hollywood's biggest stage. They say that stories like this only happen in the movies. I cannot believe it is happening to me. This is the American dream."

Recent surveys suggest that the American dream is working out for some and not for others. At first glance, it seems Americans

[1] "Read Martin Luther King Jr.'s 'I Have a Dream' Speech in Its Entirety," NPR, January 16, 2023, https://www.npr.org/2010/01/18/122701268/i-have-a-dream-speech-in-its-entirety.

[2] Dionardo PIzana, "Remembering Dr. Martin Luther King, Jr's Beloved Community," Michigan State University Extension, March 19, 2018.

are increasingly unlikely to believe that those who work hard will get ahead and that their children will be better off than they are. A 2023 poll by *The Wall Street Journal* asked respondents whether they believe the American dream is still true, that if you work hard you will get ahead in life. Only 36 percent of the respondents said it does hold true, while 18 percent said it never held true, and 45 percent said it once held true but not anymore. Americans over the generations have tended to be better off than their parents, another metric by which the American dream could be measured. Americans appear to be increasingly worried that this trend won't hold going forward.[3]

Yet a majority of Latinos (60 percent) in the U.S. say they can still attain the American dream. In fact, an Axios-Ipsos Latino Poll taken after two years of the pandemic indicates that 94 percent believe that hard work and an ability to speak English will enable them to succeed. Ipsos pollster Chris Jackson suggests that the findings show that Latinos are generally optimistic that they can transcend even barriers like racism and poverty,[4]

Is the American dream in peril? John F. Early and Phil Gramm of *The Wall Street Journal* report that upward mobility is alive and well in the United States. They say studies show that the vast majority of adults actually have higher income than their parents did. Analysts for the Pew Charitable Trusts compared the inflation-adjusted income of parents with that of their children some thirty years later. They found that 93 percent of children who grew up the bottom income quintile were better off than their parents, that 86 percent of middle-class children grew up to live in families with higher incomes than their parents, and that even 70 percent those in the top income quintile were better off. Their report concludes: "It is better to be born rich, brilliant and beautiful, but poor, ordinary and homely people succeed in America every day. The American Dream is alive and well."[5]

---

[3] Dave Lawler, "Americans Think the American Dream Is Dying," *Axios*, November 25, 2023.

[4] Russell Contreras, "Exclusive Poll: Most Latinos Believe in the American Dream," *Axios*, March 24, 2022.

[5] John F. Early and Phil Gramm, "Upward Mobility Is Alive and Well in America," *The Wall Street Journal*, January 6, 2023.

The American dream has often been measured by financial gain and the achievements of successive generations. But what about the dream of societal progress measured in terms of social justice where there is equal opportunity for all? Where refugees and migrant families are not called criminals but rather treated with compassion and acceptance? Where fellow citizens respect one another and work together for the common good? How do we reclaim the promise of the great American experiment?

Religious Views of Immigration

Angels Unawares, a bronze sculpture by Timothy Schmalz, depicts a large raft crowded with 140 figures of migrants from various nations. It was installed in St. Peter's Square in the Vatican in 2019 to mark the 105th World Migrant and Refugee Day. Pope Francis led a prayer service for migrants and refugees in front of the statue on October 19, 2023, during the sixteenth general assembly of the synod of bishops. In his homily the pope called for immigration reform with heart, drawing from the lesson of Jesus' parable of the good Samaritan. Referencing the millions of migrants and refugees forced to travel far from their homelands and often exploited along the way, Pope Francis said:

> The road leading from Jerusalem to Jericho was not a safe route, just as today the many migration routes that traverse deserts, forests, rivers and seas are not safe ... How many of our brothers and sisters find themselves today in the same condition as the traveler in the parable? How many are robbed, stripped and beaten along the way? ... The migration routes of our time are filled with men and women who are wounded and left half-dead, our brothers and sisters whose pain cries out before God.[6]

According to the *National Catholic Reporter*, the pope, in his pastoral remarks,

> called for the reform of immigration policies to increase regular, legal channels for migration, recognizing national economic and demographic policies, but always putting

[6] Cindy Wooden, "At Synod Prayer Service, Pope Calls for Immigration Reform with Heart," *National Catholic Reporter*, October 19, 2023.

> 'the most vulnerable at the center.' And, he said, those policies should recognize the benefits migrants bring to their new homelands, including 'the growth of more inclusive, more beautiful and more peaceful societies.'[7]

While Pope Francis was urging compassion and mercy in his call for reform, religious groups in the United States were all over the map in their view of migrants and immigration reform. A comprehensive research survey on American attitudes toward immigration conducted by the Public Religion Research Institute reveals some conflicting opinions among various religious groups in America:

> A majority of Americans (55%) say the growing number of newcomers from other countries strengthens American society, while four in ten (40%) say the growing number of newcomers from other countries threatens traditional American customs and values. Among religious groups surveyed, white Christians are the most likely to think that newcomers threaten traditional American customs and values. This includes about two-thirds of white evangelical Protestants (65%), a slim majority of white mainline Protestants (53%) and half of white Catholics (50%). By contrast, four in ten other Christians (40%) and about three in ten Hispanic Catholics (31%), Black Protestants (29%), religiously unaffiliated Americans (27%), and members of non-Christian religions (27%) also say immigrants are a threat to American society.
>
> Majorities of almost all religious groups support allowing undocumented immigrants to become citizens, including 73% of Black Protestants, 66% of religiously unaffiliated Americans, 62% of Hispanic Catholics, 60% of members of non-Christian religions, 58% of other Christians, 54% of white mainline Protestants, and 54% of white Catholics. White evangelical Protestants stand out as the only religious group in which a majority does not support a path to citizenship for undocumented immigrants, with only

[7] Wooden, "At Synod Prayer Service."

> 42% expressing support. White evangelical Protestants are also the most likely to say undocumented immigrants should be identified and deported, with 49% expressing this view.[8]

See diagram below, and for a more detailed analysis, see Appendix F.

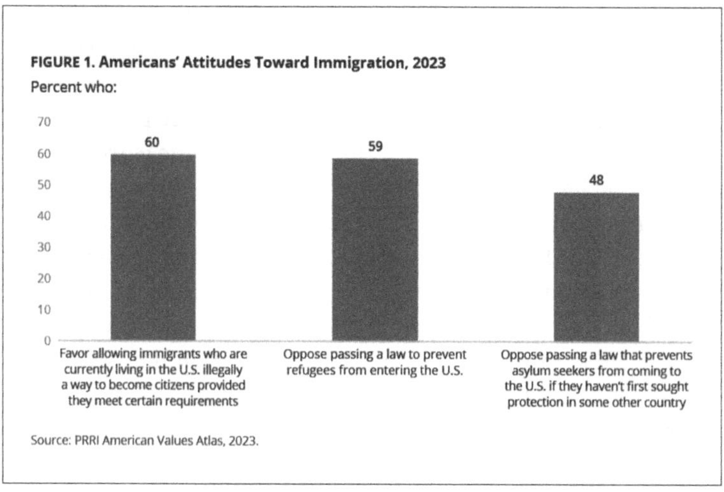

The Evangelical Lutheran Church in America (ELCA) is among one of the more progressive Christian denominations in the U.S. Seeking to be a church that embraces the stranger and, following Jesus' example, treats all people with dignity and compassion—including the refugee—the ELCA became the first sanctuary church body in the U.S. in 2019. A resolution passed at their churchwide assembly called on synods and congregations to live into the mission of welcoming and accompanying immigrants, refugees, and asylum seekers. (See Appendix C for a text of the resolution.) In their book, *They Are Us: Lutherans and Immigration*, Stephen Bouman and Ralston Deffenbaugh reflect

[8] "Are Immigrants a Threat? Most Americans Don't Think So, But Those Receptive to the 'Threat' Narrative Are Predictably More Anti-Immigrant," Public Religion Research Institute, January 17, 2023, https://www.prri.org/research/are-immigrants-a-threat-most-americans-dont-think-so-but-those-receptive-to-the-threat-narrative-are-predictably-more-anti-immigrant/.

on the traditional concept of sanctuary as a place of safety and protection. They share an explanation by ELCA synodical Bishop Jim Gonia that becoming a sanctuary denomination is about loving our neighbors by walking alongside immigrants and refugees.

According to Bishop Gonia:

> Being a sanctuary denomination will look different in different contexts. It may mean providing space for people to live; providing financial and legal support to those who are working through the immigration system; or supporting other congregations and service providers ... While we don't yet know the full scope of the work that this declaration will open for the church, we do know that our faith communities are already doing sanctuary work. Sanctuary for a congregation may mean hosting English as a Second Language (ESL) classes, marching as people of faith against the detention of children and families, providing housing for a community member facing deportation, having thoughtful conversations about what our faith says about immigration.[9]

Another ELCA synodical bishop, Shelley Bryan Wee, visited the border towns of El Paso, Texas, and Las Cruces, Arizona, in early 2024. She reported on the work of Border Servant Corps, a faith-based organization providing refuge for people seeking asylum in the U.S. in the form of food, shelter, medical care, and legal assistance. Bishop Bryan Wee reflected on how thankful she was that the church she serves has a long history of accompanying those who come from other lands. She shared a nurse's description of what motivates her work at the border: "I won't miss any opportunity I have to touch the face of Christ."[10]

The Need for Immigration Reform is Long Overdue

Immigration has been an important part of the history, tradition, and strength of the United States. For over two centuries

---

[9] Stephen Bouman and Ralston Deffenbaugh, *They Are Us: Lutherans and Immigration* (Minneapolis: Fortress Press, 2020), 190–91.

[10] Shelley Bryan Wee, Facebook,February 1, 2024, https://www.facebook.com/shelley.b.wee/posts/pfbid02uUbBQcsAnHEUxNLPmG6N-DYJBjJsR67NoKG7kU7PxUfriwYKu85SoguVx6xNas53al .

our nation has welcomed immigrants with the expectation that they would become citizens and participating members of American society. Writing for *The New York Times*, David Leonhardt suggests that even with the present "border crisis," the majority of Americans are not opposed to immigration. In fact, he notes that during Trump's presidency, the number of Americans who favored increasing immigration exceeded the number who favored decreasing it—likely in reaction to Trump's slashing immigration quotas. While that trend has again reversed itself, he writes:

> Most say that legal immigrants strengthen the country, and many believe the U.S. should remain a haven for people fleeing repression. But most Americans also think that the country's immigration laws should mean something and that citizens of other countries should not be able to enter this country simply because they want to.[11]

Most Americans agree that the current immigration crisis is the result of a broken system. And, unfortunately, efforts at comprehensive immigration reform have repeatedly failed in an increasingly polarized Congress. It seems that many Americans view foreigners with caution and suspicion, which overshadows the positive contributions of immigrants to this country. Now, as another election cycle is upon us, politicians and talk show hosts are fanning the flames and increasing the fear factor among voters by claiming that we are experiencing an invasion of unsavory characters at the border.

The 118th U.S. Congress was in a heated debate about the future of refugees and asylum seekers in early 2024. Republicans who held a majority in the House of Representatives insisted that the "border crisis" needed to be addressed, including by significant revisions to the asylum process. Responding to these concerns, the U.S. Senate proposed a bipartisan immigration reform bill that was the strictest in decades. Presidential candidate Trump—wishing to make immigration a signature campaign issue—insisted that the House reject the bill and any immigration reform. As a result,

---

[11] David Leonhardt, "A 2024 Vulnerability," *The New York Times*, January 12, 2024.

Speaker of the House Mike Johnson announced that the Senate bill was dead on arrival. The GOP Whip Tom Emmer commented, "Any deal from the Senate that allows for even ONE illegal crossing will be dead on arrival in the House."[12]

According to Krish O'Mara Vignariajah, president and CEO of Global Refuge, "what we're seeing at our southern border is essentially a global and regional humanitarian crisis that is colliding with our broken immigration system." Speaking on radio station WYPR (Baltimore), she shared her concern that proposed changes are part of a deterrence-only strategy that some lawmakers are pursuing and suggests that our leaders need to cooperate to ensure our country meets its legal and humanitarian obligations to asylum seekers at the border. "We're seeing so many migrants coming to the southern border as a result of slow-burning crises abroad combined with the fact that we have not had reform of the immigration system for three decades."[13]

This broken immigration system needs to be fixed for many reasons. Millions of both documented and undocumented immigrants, asylum seekers, and refugees lead desperate lives. This includes the suffering of those incarcerated for coming to this country without proper documentation as well as families and communities that are being torn apart. Some states have banned health and social services for the undocumented and are refusing to allow their children to attend public school. Referring to the increased ugliness of the debate over immigration, Bouman and Deffenbaugh write: "Until there is comprehensive immigration reform, there will be more and more license in America to denigrate and divide and treat certain groups of people as being less than equal, less than worthy. It does America no honor to have an underclass living in fear and subject to insult."[14]

They go on to suggest that "any immigration reform should provide a path to permanent status and citizenship for persons who put down roots in America and want to become contributing

[12] Lauren Peller, "Even Worse Than We Expected: House Speaker Reacts to Bipartisan Senate Immigration Bill," *ABC News*, February 4, 2024.

[13] Krish O'Mara Vignarajah speaking on WYPR (Baltimore), January 2, 2024.

[14] Bouman and Deffenbaugh, *They Are Us*, 93.

members of society."[15] This includes refugees and asylum seekers who are here legally, as well as the "Dreamers" who were brought here as children. And what about their parents who are undocumented? While there is a criminal statute of limitations for most crimes in this country, there is none for those who have entered illegally. Might they be judged on the merits of a productive life well lived with no criminal record?

Perhaps we should ask, "What would Jesus do?" Or rather, "How would Jesus want Americans to tackle the immigration issue?" Adam Russell Taylor, president of *Sojourners*, writes:

> After decades of congressional failure to pass comprehensive immigration reform and deliberate efforts by the former Trump administration to dismantle the system, we're left with an immigration system that is fundamentally broken. We don't have enough judges or aid workers to process asylum claims and we don't have enough shelters where migrants can wait while their asylum claims are processed. Nonprofits like the Red Cross, and faith-based organization like Catholic Charities and Church World Service, provide vital services to fill many of these gaps, but these groups cannot meet all the needs of the migrants at their doors. The result of all this is an estimated backlog of 2 million cases and yearslong delays. When you combine an overburdened system with a record number of new migrants seeking asylum, you get the current crisis, which can easily feel intractable. What does Jesus call us to do in a moment like this?[16]

Believing that Jesus always calls us to protect the inherent dignity of migrants, Taylor not only calls on Congress to pass comprehensive immigration reform legislation, but also suggests that our faith enables us to imagine a new immigration system in which many of the root causes of migration, such as extreme poverty, violence, and conflict, are redressed. He concludes: "As the church in the U.S., let us amplify the voices of migrants and speak

---

[15] Bouman and Deffenbaugh, *They Are Us*, 49.

[16] Adam Russell Taylor, "Jesus Wants Dignity for Migrants. U.S. Policy? Not So Much," *Sojourners*, May 18, 2023.

up for immigration policies that protect the life and dignity of those who knock at our nation's doorstep seeking safety and freedom."[17]

What Will It Take to Reclaim the Promise of the American Dream?

At a moment in which our nation seems more divided than at the time of the Civil War, when threats and acts of violence against various ethnic groups and members of the LGBTQ community have substantially increased, and when the Southern Poverty Law Center reports that in 2023 there were over 1,200 domestic hate groups in the U.S., how do we find a way to come together for the common good? More than immigration reform is needed in order to transform the American spirit, to restore the values of civility, goodness, generosity, and compassion. How do we go about embracing the beautiful tapestry of diversity that makes our nation extraordinary? Let us explore five ways that could help us move beyond our polarization and our suspicion or hatred of the other, to embrace one another as God's beloved children.

WAY ONE: Love the Neighbor

A church reader board displayed the following: "LOVE YOUR NEIGHBOR WHO DOESN'T: look like you, think like you, love like you, speak like you, pray like you, vote like you. LOVE YOUR NEIGHBOR. NO EXCEPTIONS." I suspect Jesus would concur. Matthew writes in his gospel of an incident in which a lawyer asks Jesus, "What is the greatest commandment?" Jesus replies: "`Love the Lord your God with all your heart and with all your soul and with all your mind.' This is the first and greatest commandment. And the second is like it: `Love your neighbor as yourself'" (Mt. 22:36–40).

Jesus tells his disciples when they are gathered for the Last Supper: "I give you a new commandment, that you love one another. Just as I have loved you, you also should love one another. By this everyone will know that you are my disciples, if you have love for one another" (John 13:34–35). The sixteenth-century theologian and reformer Martin Luther suggested that the *neighbor* was not

[17] Taylor, "Jesus Wants Dignity for Migrants."

just the person next door or a close friend but the one in need, the downtrodden one, the sojourner, and people on the margins.

At the wedding of Prince Harry and Meghan Markle, Michael Curry, presiding bishop of the Episcopal Church, offered his take on what it means to live a life of love for others. He reflected on the New Testament scripture from 1 John 4:7–8: "Beloved, let us love one another, because love is from God; everyone who loves is born of God and knows God. Whoever does not love does not know God, for God is love." Then he invited those gathered to imagine a world where love is the way:

> Imagine our homes and families where love is the way. Imagine neighborhoods and communities where love is the way. Imagine governments and nations where love is the way. Imagine business and commerce where this love is the way. Imagine this tired old world where love is the way. When love is the way—unselfish, sacrificial, redemptive. When love is the way, then no child will go to bed hungry in this world ever again. When love is the way, we will let justice roll down like a mighty stream and righteousness like an ever-flowing brook. When love is the way, poverty will become history. When love is the way, the earth will be a sanctuary. When love is the way, we will lay down our swords and shields, down by the riverside, to study war no more. When love is the way, there's plenty good room—plenty good room—for all of God's children. Because when love is the way, we actually treat each other like we are actually family. When love is the way, we know that God is the source of us all, and we are brothers and sisters, children of God. My brothers and sisters, that's a new heaven, a new earth, a new world, a new human family.[18]

WAY TWO: Try Civil Discourse

We know what people mean when they talk of the *red state, blue state divide*. In our current polarized climate, there is evidence

---

[18] Maquita Peters, "Bishop Michael Curry's Royal Wedding Sermon: Full Text of 'The Power of Love,'", *NPR*, May 20, 2018, https://www.npr.org/sections/thetwo-way/2018/05/20/612798691/bishop-michael-currys-royal-wedding-sermon-full-text-of-the-power-of-love.

that we may have lost the ability to be civil or courteous with one another. The polarization of politics and the cultural division in our country has poisoned our public discourse. We seem to have discarded societal norms such as civility, decency, integrity, kindness, and even common courtesy and replaced them with distrust and contempt. Instead of trying to understand those who disagree with us, we are motivated to marginalize or defeat them.

It seems that anyone who is not of our "tribe" is suspect and we may feel threatened by them. There is the tendency to dismiss another's point of view or even demonize them because they are not like us. It is okay to disagree with someone, but it's not okay to dehumanize or denigrate them. There must be a way to have authentic conversation without always questioning the motives of others. Perhaps we need to relearn the art of agreeing to disagree. And rather than being defensive or accusatory, we could try to really listen to one another. In so doing we might find those areas where we actually agree on something. We could even discover that we share some common values and mutual hopes.

A number of organizations have appeared on the scene as a result of the current climate to help bring people together, even those who are polar opposites, for the purpose of having meaningful, civil conversation. It's their attempt to try and bridge the divide. One such organization is called Braver Angels. Their tagline: "We are a citizens' organization uniting red and blue Americans in a working alliance to depolarize America." They have chapters all over the country, which sponsor forums and offer workshops in an effort to bring people together. A new organization is Starts With Us, which seeks to "empower the 87% of Americans frustrated with extreme political and cultural divisions with the skills to engage across our differences and move our country forward." They offer inspiring stories, practical tips, and ways to take action." (For more information on these organizations and for their contact information, see Appendix B.)

WAY 3: Practice Compassion

Compassion and kindness have often been hallmarks of the American culture. Our nation is known for its generosity in reaching out to help hurting people domestically and all over the globe following a disaster. We have excelled in lifting people up in response to a hardship. Consider the following story about how an interfaith group responded to a political ploy with grace and compassion.

In June 2022, Governor Ron DeSantis signed a budget earmarking $12 million to "facilitate the transport of unauthorized aliens out of Florida." The following June, a flight from Florida arrived in Sacramento; aboard were sixteen asylum seekers from Venezuela. Other flights to California's capital would soon follow with more migrants. Gabby Trejo was the executive director of SacACT, a branch of a national interfaith organization called Faith in Action. A Catholic and an immigrant herself, she believed this situation was a call to put faith into practice. She enlisted Fr. Juan Francisco Bracamontes-Monjaraz, the pastor of Sacramento's Our Lady of Guadalupe parish. He opened the doors of his church as makeshift accommodation for the migrants for as long as they needed. She then turned to Rabbi Mona Alfi, leader of congregation B'nai Israel, which had experience working with refugees. His congregation had voted several years earlier to declare themselves a "sanctuary congregation," meaning its members are "ready to provide shelter when we are called upon." Trinity Episcopal Cathedral and Parkside Community Church also soon got involved, offering food, shelter, clothing, and other needed services. One of the migrants interviewed by the media responded: "I have no words. They offered true support, substantial support. I feel very lucky, very blessed. I thank God for putting these people in my path."[19]

Compassion is central to the Christian understanding of God. While the Hebrew scriptures describe God as compassionate, in the person of Jesus we have an incarnational expression of compassion. This is the God made flesh who comes to dwell among us and to share in our sufferings. Compassion implies the capacity of one to enter into places of pain with others, and according to the apostle Paul "to weep with those who weep" (Romans 12:15). God calls those who follow Jesus to show mercy and compassion "to the least of these" (Matthew 25:40). According to Rev. Ben Cremer,

[19] Ethan Bauer, "The Shepherds of Sacramento, CA," *The Commonweal*, January 5, 2024.

campus pastor at the Cathedral of the Rockies: "Matthew 25 tells us that when Jesus returns and judges between the righteous and unrighteous, he doesn't judge them based on their orthodoxy, their patriotism, or their individual definitions of morality. He judges them based on their compassion towards vulnerable people."[20]

There are many ways that one might show compassion and kindness to others. One could sponsor a refugee family or foster a refugee child. Or volunteer at the local community food bank, etc. Every community is looking for volunteers who can help the less fortunate among us.

WAY 4: Live with a Spirit of Generosity

"Is the glass half full or half empty?" We've all heard that question. Our response tells how one views one's circumstances in life. It describes an attitude that affects our outlook in either a positive or negative way. If we see the glass usually as "half-empty," we may consider ourselves unfortunate or unlucky. We may believe our resources and opportunities to be limited. Those who view the glass as always "half full" tend to have a more optimistic outlook on life. They are able to see the possibilities, they recognize their many blessings, and are often eager to share of their abundance with others. The reality is that most of us can afford to be generous.

America is often considered the richest nation in the world. It is true that even the poor among us are considered "well off" by the world's standards. Unless one has traveled to second- or third-world countries, one cannot appreciate how blessed one is to live in the United States. And here lies the problem. We think that if we let others into our country to partake of a share in its wealth, there will be less available for the nation's citizens. What we fail to realize is that not only is there enough to go around, but that when the lowest among us rise up, the rest of us rise up as well. The country is richer because of the gifts and resources that we all bring to the table. We have a choice: we can live with a theology of scarcity or a theology of abundance, a theology of despair or a theology of hope.

---

[20] Rev. Benjamin Cremer, Twitter, February 3, 2022, https://twitter.com/Brcremer/status/1489236162623389697.

At a time when there was an isolationist attitude in Congress and America seemed to be turning inward, Britain's prime minister, Tony Blair, gave a major address to the Economic Club of Chicago in April 1999. He offered his hope for America: "Stay, please, a country outward-looking with the vision and the imagination which is the very best of your nature. And realize, too, that in doing so, you fashion the design of a future built on peace and prosperity for all, which is the only dream that makes humanity worth preserving."[21]

WAY 5: Embrace Diversity

The YMCA welcome sign exemplifies diversity and inclusion. Posted in most Y lobbies, it reads: "WE WELCOME ALL races, ALL religions, ALL countries of origin, ALL sexual orientations, ALL genders. Let's be fearless." This sign reminds us that we are all God's children and, as such, we are all worthy of dignity and respect. Furthermore, we are all connected with one another, with God, and with all creation. Twentieth-century German theologian Dietrich Bonhoeffer used the German word "Gottesgemeinschaft," which literally means "God's community." He wrote that we are a community of God, human beings, and God's creatures. As, such we have a collective responsibility. When we tear it down, we are in Adam. When we build it up, we are in Christ. The essence of sin is when we isolate ourselves from one another. When we seek to exclude rather than include people from our community, we fail to understand our connection or relationship with others and need to repent of our brokenness. For Bonhoeffer, the church was the "sanctorum communion," a community that represents Christ's promise of a new humanity and a sign of peace, justice, and hope and love.[22]

Adam Russell Taylor, in his book *A More Perfect Union: A New Vision for Building the Beloved Community*, writes:

> America's strength does not derive from an assimilating uniformity but instead from the richness of authentic

[21] Rob D. Kaiser and Michael McGuire, "Blair Unveils Bold Intervention Doctrine," *The Chicago Tribune*, April 23, 1999.

[22] David M. Elcott, *Faith, Nationalism and the Future of Liberal Democracy*, (Notre Dame, IN: University of Notre Dame Press, 2021), 126.

> expressions of diversity ... Our oneness is also not found in a single culture, language, or place of origin but rather in our shared ideals, values, and aspirations, as well as in our commitment to love the other as much as ourselves.

He wonders if America is truly a people in addition to being a nation:

> How do we combine the best of our distinctive racial and ethnic cultures with a shared sense of peoplehood rooted in an embrace of our beautiful diversity? ... Becoming one people and one nation requires that we make a firm choice in favor of embracing a multiracial, multireligious democracy. This requires letting go of the notion that white and/or Christian America is the true America and that America is only for certain types of people ... Our aim should be to build an America that is antiracist, committed to building the Beloved Community.[23]

Conclusion

The American dream continues to be a driving force for immigration to this country. However, since the founding of the nation, there have been two competing visions for what this country is intended to be and for whom it is intended. Is America a kind of promised land for European Christians? Or is America a pluralistic democracy, where everyone—regardless of race, religion, sexual orientation, or other characteristics—stands on equal footing as citizens?[24] It seems the latter would be more in keeping with God's vision for true community and what the founders intended when they sought to form a more perfect union.

Throughout our history individuals as well as cultural forces have sought to divide us as a people. Would that we could defy them and embrace a united vision for our future! The *Boys in the Boat* is a story about the University of Washington crew team, which won the gold medal at the 1936 Olympics in Berlin. To succeed took grit and determination. But, more than that, the members of the

[23] Adam Russell Taylor, *A More Perfect Union: A New Vision for Building the Beloved Community* (Minneapolis: Broadleaf Books, 2021), 32–39.

[24] Questions attributed to Robert Jones, author of *The Hidden Roots of White Supremacy and the Path to a Shared American Future.*

crew had to learn how to become one with each other and with their boat. It was their trust in each other, their mutual respect, humility, and sense of fair play that enabled them to do so. Their belief in one another and their willingness to sacrifice for the other enabled them to become a winning team. This is a parable for what our country needs today.

America is a rich tapestry of many different peoples representing myriad ethnic groups, cultures, lifestyles, and religions. This is what makes us great as a country. This is also a vision of God's beloved community. This is the promise of America. When we recognize and embrace this truth, that all people, including newcomers, are welcome and have the opportunity to thrive, our nation will have a future of hope as described in the following song:

Build a longer table, not a higher wall,
feeding those who hunger, making room for all.
Feasting together, stranger turns to friend,
Christ breaks walls to pieces, false divisions end.
Build a safer refuge, not a larger jail.
Where the weak find shelter, mercy will not fail.
For any place where justice is denied,
Christ will breach the wall, freeing all inside.
Build a broader doorway, not a longer fence,
love protects all people, sparing no expense.
When we embrace compassion more than fear,
Christ tears down our fences, all are welcome here.
When we lived as exiles, refugees abroad,
Christ became our doorway to the reign of God.
So must our tables welcome those who roam.
None can be excluded, all must find a home.[25]

Mother Francis Xavier Cabrini (1850–1917) was the first U.S. citizen to be canonized a saint by the Roman Catholic Church. The movie *Cabrini* chronicles her life and the work of the order she founded, the Missionary Sisters of the Sacred Heart of Jesus. They established numerous orphanages, schools, and hospitals in

---

[25] David Bjorlin, "Build a Longer Table" (GIA Publications Inc., 2018).

America and around the world. Their acts of courage, kindness, and compassion brought solace and hope to countless refugees and others. In 1950, Pope Pius XII named Cabrini the patron saint of immigrants. At the end of the 2024 film, we are left to ponder two questions: What kind of a world do we wish to live in? What are we willing to do to achieve that dream?

QUESTIONS FOR REFLECTION:

1. How do you think Martin Luther King Jr. envisioned the American dream? How do you understand the American dream, and do you think it is still possible to achieve it?

2. What strikes you about the different religious attitudes toward immigration?

3. Do you believe the immigration system is broken? If so, how is it broken, and what might be done to fix it?

4. Consider the five ways suggested to restore the promise of America. How would you rank them in order of importance? What are some steps that you are your congregation might take to advance the promise of America?

5 .What are your thoughts about the two competing visions for America suggested in the Conclusion?

6,. Describe your hope for America's future.

Appendix A

Immigration Organizations

Resettlement Agencies that Partner with UNHCR, the UN Refugee Agency

Bethany Christian Services (since 1944)
901 Eastern Ave. NE., Grand Rapids, MI 49503
Phone: 800-238-4269
Website: Bethany.org

Church World Service (since 1946)
475 Riverside Dr., Suite 700, New York, NY, 10115
Phone: 212-870-2061, 800-297-1516
Website: CWSglobal.org

Episcopal Migration Ministries (since the 1980s)
815 Second Ave., New York, NY, 10017
Phone: 212-716-6000, 800-334-7626
Website: EpiscopalChurch.org/ministries/episcopal-migration-ministries/

Ethiopian Community Development Council (since 1983)
901 S. Highland St., Arlington, VA 22204
Phone: 703-685-0510, ext. 224
Website: EEDCUS.org

Global Refugee/Lutheran Immigration and Refugee Services (since 1939)
700 Light St., Baltimore, MD 21297
Phone: 410-983-4000
Website: GlobalRefuge.org

Hebrew Immigrant Aid Society (since 1903)
1300 Spring St., Suite 500, Silver Spring, MD 20910
Phone: 301-844-7300
Website: HIAS.org

International Rescue Committee (IRC) (since 1933)
U.S. Office: 1200 S. 192nd St., Suite 101, SeaTac, WA 98148
Phone: 206-623-2105
Website: Rescue.org

United States Conference of Catholic Bishops (since the 1980s)
Refugee Resettlement Services: 939 E. Park Dr., Suite 102, Harrisburg, PA 17111
Phone: 717-232-0568, ext. 204
Website: USCCB.org

U.S. Committee for Refugees and Immigrants (since 1911)
2231 Crystal Dr., Suite 350, Arlington, VA
Phone: 703-310-1130
Website: Refugees.org

World Relief Corporation (since 1944)
7 E. Baltimore St., Baltimore, MD 21202
Phone: 443-451-1900
Website: WorldRelief.org
For more information about the work of the UN Refugee Agency, check out the following link: https://www.unhcr.org/us/what-we-do/resettlement-united-states/u-s-resettlement-partners.

Appendix B

Resources For Civil Discourse

Braver Angels

Website: BraverAngels.org

"We bring Americans together to bridge the partisan divide and strengthen our democratic republic."

Listen First Coalition

Website: ListenFirstProject.org/listen-first-coalition

"400+ organizations bringing Americans together across differences to listen, understand each other, and discover common interests."

Resetting the Table

Website: ResettingtheTable.org

Courageous communication across divides.

"Supporting collaborative deliberation in the face of strong differences."

Starts With Us

Website: StartsWith.us

Overcoming extreme division starts with us!

"Starts With Us is a movement to overcome political and cultural divisions in America by practicing curiosity, compassion, and courage every day."

Appendix C

ELCA Resolution: A Sanctuary Church

Reprinted with permission of the Evangelical Lutheran Church in America.

The Evangelical Lutheran Church in America (ELCA) becomes a sanctuary denomination. The 2019 ELCA Churchwide Assembly voted to approve a memorial that affirms the denomination's long-standing commitment to migrants and refugees and declares the Evangelical Lutheran Church in America (ELCA) a sanctuary church body. The ELCA was the first North American denomination to declare itself a sanctuary church body. As a sanctuary church, the ELCA publicly declared that walking alongside immigrants and refugees is a matter of faith. This declaration does not call for any person, congregation, or synod to engage in illegal activity. Below is the text of the memorial originally submitted by The Metropolitan New York Synod of the ELCA.

Overview of the Sanctuary Movement

Christians have offered sanctuary for two thousand years, continuing an ancient biblical practice in which cities and houses of worship provided refuge and asylum for people fleeing injustice. Started in the 1980s, the Sanctuary Movement was a faith-based initiative to protect Central American refugees fleeing civil war and seeking safety in the U.S. Today, the New Sanctuary Movement is a revived effort for communities of faith to walk alongside immigrants in the U.S.

While there is no uniform definition of sanctuary, its overall purpose is to faithfully and openly act to ensure that all feel safe and welcomed. The ways in which sanctuary is provided vary by congregation, but it can include providing physical shelter to a community member at risk of deportation, inviting and welcoming all to worship regardless of immigration status, providing services to migrants, responding to raids or other emergencies, aiding all regardless of immigration status and actively advocating for migrants. These activities are completely legal and are born of our faith traditions.

One controversial activity that some sanctuary congregations engage in is physically hosting a community member at risk of deportation. While there are varied views as to the interpretation of the law, knowingly concealing, harboring, or shielding (or attempting to conceal, harbor, or shield) an undocumented immigrant from detection by the authorities is illegal. Similarly, knowingly transporting or moving (or attempting to transport or move) an undocumented immigrant from one place to another, where the transportation helps the immigrant remain in the US unlawfully, violates the law. Congregations or individuals that engage in legally controversial practices often view their actions as civil disobedience—knowingly violating a law to shine a light on its injustice. Civil disobedience also has an important and rich history in faith traditions all over the world, but civil disobedience includes accepting the consequences that naturally flow from breaking the law.

Thus, sanctuary is a broad term that is applied to a variety of practices, most of which are legal.

ELCA Sanctuary Timeline

Lutherans have a long history of standing alongside immigrants and refugees through church ministries or by connecting with Lutheran Immigration and Refugee Service (LIRS).

Congregations in predecessor bodies of the Evangelical Lutheran Church in America (ELCA) were essential in the sanctuary movement during the 1980s. Today, ELCA congregations, including Angelica Lutheran Church in Los Angeles and Lutheran Church of the Good Shepherd in Brooklyn, NY, have independently joined the New Sanctuary Movement through their local networks. Notably, Augustana Lutheran Church in Portland, OR gave sanctuary in 2014 to Francisco Aguirre, a migrant from

El Salvador facing deportation. Currently at least two ELCA congregations, and probably more, are providing sanctuary. Recently, Gethsemane Lutheran, Seattle, saw Jose Robles, who has been in sanctuary in its church for almost a year, taken into custody following an US Immigration and Customs Enforcement check-in appointment.

In response to the increasing numbers of unaccompanied children arriving in this country starting in 2011, the 2016 ELCA Churchwide Assembly passed the AMMPARO (Accompanying Migrant Minors with Protection, Advocacy, Representation and Opportunities) strategy.

AMMPARO recommits the church to accompanying migrant children and families in the US, in the countries of origin and in transit. Through AMMPARO, ELCA churches can become Welcoming Congregations by committing to accompanying migrants in their community through service and advocacy. While there is no central database of individual sanctuary churches, those wanting to tap into the AMMPARO network have been welcomed to do so by joining the list of Welcoming Congregations without having to take additional steps.

In May 2016, shortly before the AMMPARO strategy was adopted, the Oregon Synod passed a resolution declaring itself the first sanctuary synod in the ELCA. This resolution, which called on the ELCA to become a sanctuary denomination, was memorialized at the 2016 Churchwide Assembly. In May 2019, the Metropolitan New York Synod, itself a sanctuary synod, memorialized the 2019 Churchwide Assembly to declare itself a sanctuary church body. The 2019 Churchwide Assembly adopted a modified version of this memorial on Aug. 7. Sanctuary synods and congregations in the ELCA. During the 2017 assembly season, four additional synods declared themselves sanctuary synods: Sierra Pacific, Southwest California, New England, and Metropolitan New York (through its Synod Council). All four synods, together with the Oregon Synod, relate to AMMPARO. Further, there are ELCA congregations that have declared themselves sanctuary congregations and also consider themselves part of the AMMPARO network.

Research on sanctuary in other denominations:

Summary of findings

To understand the realities and implications of sanctuary, ELCA Advocacy interviewed staff responsible for articulating the movement and equipping churches in their contexts. The ELCA Advocacy interviewed staff from The United Methodist Church (UMC), the Episcopal Church, and the Presbyterian Church (U.S.A.). The interviews took place in June 2017 and were recently updated.

Overall, we found that the none of the three churches are sanctuary denominations, but they all encourage their congregations to make their own decisions regarding their involvement with sanctuary. For The UMC, any policies and laws attempting to limit or restrain its work of responding to the needs of others are contrary to its most fundamental beliefs as stated in the gospel. According to Resolution 6028 (adopted in 2008), the church's response to migration assistance includes recognizing "the right of sanctuary in any United Methodist local church for migrants subject to detention or deportation by government security forces." The UMC urges churches and members to commit to opposing these types of laws and encourages congregations to prayerfully choose to affirm the New Sanctuary Movement. In practice, this means disseminating resources to congregations that want to know how to become sanctuaries and continuing the UMC Immigration Task Force, which works on action and analysis of the policy realities affecting migrants.

The General Assembly of the Presbyterian Church (U.S.A.) has supported congregations and members participating in the Sanctuary Movement since its inception in the 1980s. The church states it will open congregations and communities as sanctuary spaces for those targeted by hate, to ensure the human rights of all people. The denomination has not declared sanctuary status, but supports congregations in doing so as witness on the behalf of immigrants. In 2016, a resolution was passed reaffirming the ministry of sanctuary and the support of congregations that have provided sanctuary for immigrants and refugees. The resolution also calls for congregations and individuals to advocate and organize "for humanitarian, just immigration policies on the local, state, and federal levels." Through this, the Presbyterian Church provides resources, including legal resources, to help individuals be informed on how to assist. Most of the pushback received on the resolution language has been a minority voice.

The Episcopal Church's most recent resolution in 2018, titled "Becoming a Sanctuary Church," affirms the New Sanctuary Movement; urges its members to advocacy for unjust policies; recommends that its congregations be places of sanctuary; encourages its members to connect with local sanctuary movements; and, as a church body, calls for advocacy for such things as comprehensive immigration reform. The church encourages dioceses and congregations to commit to protecting migrants but, similarly to The UMC and Presbyterian Church, does not declare itself a sanctuary denomination. In practice, the extent to which the dioceses commit to the recent resolution vary, but Los Angeles and New Jersey dioceses for example, have declared themselves sanctuary dioceses.

In conclusion, while none of the ELCA's full communion partners in this report have become a sanctuary denomination, at least three support the New Sanctuary Movement overall. As in the ELCA memorial, the decision on how congregations and individuals would like to participate is up to the discretion of each synod and congregation.

Conclusions and next steps

The ELCA, in all its expressions, has a long-documented history of standing alongside migrants and refugees. Recognizing that our confidence in God's grace leads us to engage immigration issues differently, and that in a political climate where migrants and refugees are aggressively targeted for deportation and depicted often as security threats, it is imperative for all faith communities to be vocal about our belief that people are created in God's image, worthy of dignity and safety. Sanctuary has been an interfaith expression of the commitment of faith communities to welcome the stranger.

The ELCA already has a number of pathways for churches and congregants to provide services, advocate, and welcome immigrants through synod immigration task forces, AMMPARO, and LIRS. Synod task forces, LIRS, AMMPARO, and formal churchwide actions already call on churches to walk alongside migrants and become part of a Lutheran network working with migrant communities in different capacities. To complement these networks, the ELCA has now expressed its support for sanctuary and is calling on churches to be involved in activities to protect migrants through our existing networks. Through ELCA AMMPARO, we:

1. Encourage ELCA congregations and synods to learn about and support the New Sanctuary Movement in their area, which is often manifest as an ecumenical or interfaith effort.

2. Provide educational and practical resources and information for congregations as they consider their part in providing sanctuary, including ways for them to understand possible legal risks.

3. Gather the five sanctuary synods in consultation with AMMPARO, learn from them and find best practices that can guide the ELCA as a sanctuary denomination.

4. Encourage synod immigration task forces and AMMPARO groups to be engaged with the movement in their area and accompany the work on local migrant community organizations.

5. Call on all congregations, including current sanctuary congregations, to support the spirit of the New Sanctuary Movement by serving the migrant communities around them, becoming Welcoming Congregations and/or sanctuary congregations, and joining the AMMPARO movement. There is a place for everyone in AMMPARO.

QUESTIONS FOR REFLECTION:

1. What do you believe is the significance of this action by this church body?

2. What do you think could be the impact of such a statement?

3. What questions or concerns does this raise for you as it relates to the current challenges of immigration in America today?

Appendix D

Repudiation Of The Doctrine Of Discovery

(Evangelical Lutheran Church in America)

This social policy was adopted by the ELCA Churchwide Assembly in 2016. It is reprinted here with permission of the Evangelical Lutheran Church in America.

ACTION CA16.02.04

To receive with gratitude memorials from the Alaska, Northwest Washington, Montana, Southwest California, Rocky Mountain, Eastern North Dakota, South Dakota, Minneapolis Area, Saint Paul Area, Arkansas-Oklahoma, Northwest Wisconsin, East-Central Wisconsin, Indiana-Kentucky, Update New York, Northwestern Pennsylvania, Metropolitan Washington, D.C., North Carolina and Southeastern synods regarding the Repudiation of the Doctrine of Discovery;

To repudiate explicitly and clearly the European-derived doctrine of discovery as an example of the "improper mixing of the power of the church and the power of the sword" (Augsburg Confession Article XXVIII, Latin text), and to acknowledge and repent from this church's complicity in the evils of colonialism in the Americas, which continue to harm tribal governments and individual tribal members;

To offer a statement of repentance and reconciliation to native nations in this country for damage done in the name of Christianity;

To encourage the Office of the Presiding Bishop to plan an appropriate national ceremony of repentance and reconciliation with tribal leaders, providing appropriate worship resources for similar synodical and congregational observances with local tribal leaders, at such times and places as are appropriate;

To direct the Domestic Mission unit, together with the American Indian and Alaska Native community and ecumenical partners, to develop resources to educate members of the ELCA and the wider community about the doctrine of discovery and its consequences for native peoples;

To direct the Domestic Mission unit to develop a strategy with the American Indian and Alaska Native community during the next triennium to be referred to the Church Council for action, including a mechanism to grow the Native American Ministry Fund of the ELCA; and

To affirm that this church will eliminate the doctrine of discovery from its contemporary rhetoric and programs, electing to practice accompaniment with native peoples instead of a missionary endeavor to them, allowing these partnerships to mutually enrich indigenous communities and the ministries of the ELCA.

QUESTIONS FOR REFLECTION:

1. What do you believe is the significance of this action by this church body?

2. What do you think could be the impact of such a statement?

3. What questions or concerns does this raise for you as it relates to the current challenges of immigration in America today?

Appendix E

Repudiation Of The Doctrine Of Discovery (Disciples Of Christ)

Reprinted with permission of the Christian Church (Disciples of Christ).

Repudiation Of The Christian Doctrine Of Discovery: A Call To Education And Action, And Support For Indigenous Voices In The Witness Of The Christian Church (Disciples Of Christ)

(1) **WHEREAS,** Luke 4:16–21(NRSV) testifies to the 5-fold mission of Jesus Christ to "bring good news to the poor, proclaim release to the captives, recovery of sight to the blind, and let the oppressed go free, and proclaim the year of the Lord's favor" thereby calling Jesus' disciples to oppose genocide, oppression, dehumanization, and the removal of Peoples from ancestral lands; and

(2) **WHEREAS**, the Christian Doctrine of Discovery (CDoD) is a body of work beginning in the 15th century with a series of papal bulls and theological statements justifying the Age of Discovery and the colonization, conquest, subjugation of lands and peoples around the world[i]: and

(3) **WHEREAS**, the Christian Doctrine of Discovery continues to facilitate genocide, oppression, dehumanization, and the removal of Peoples from ancestral lands in the United States, Canada and globally; and

(4) **WHEREAS**, the United States Supreme Court legally adopted the Doctrine of Discovery in the 1823 landmark decision of *Johnson v.* McIntosh [i]; and

(5) **WHEREAS**, the Christian Church (Disciples of Christ) (DOC) has historically and consistently claimed an identity

of a westward movement church on the North American Landscape; and

(6) **WHEREAS**, the DOC recognizes [that] its identity, polity, congregations, and theology have benefited from the CDoD and its legal/theological support of seizing indigenous lands and human rights abuses of indigenous peoples and further recognizes North American DOC congregations reside on land immorally acquired from Indigenous North American Tribes and Bands; and

(7) **WHEREAS**, the Christian Church (Disciples of Christ) under the guise of civilization and Christianization, engaged in programmatic assimilation, discrimination, subjugation, and desecration of Indigenous American Tribes and Bands (e.g., American Tepee Christian Mission—*also known as Yakama Christian Mission*); and

(8) **WHEREAS**, cultural, communal, and individual damage experienced by American Indians, Alaska Natives and First Nations people are disproportionate in the United States and Canada [ii]; and

(9) **WHEREAS**, governmental and economic institutions lack the will to dismantle the CDoD, and the Church is the one institution who can clearly speak against this unjust CDoD system, as it has in the past against slavery and apartheid; and

(10) **WHEREAS**, the DOC has recognized disproportionate hurt inflicted upon People of Color and oppressed Creation with Sense of the Assembly Resolutions [iii]; and

(11) **WHEREAS**, many of our ecumenical partners have already repudiated and renounced the CDOD [iv]; and

(12) **WHEREAS**, Robert Brock, Northwest Regional Minister, began a process of relational change between the DOC, American Indians, and First Nation peoples in 1987 by signing *A Public Declaration* of formal apology for the Northwest Christian Church's participation in the destruction of Native American spiritual practices;

(1) **THEREFORE, BE IT RESOLVED** the General Assembly of the Christian Church (Disciples of Christ) in the United States and Canada, meeting July 8–12, 2017, in Indianapolis, Indiana, condemns and repudiates the Christian Doctrine of Discovery; and

(2) **BE IT FURTHER RESOLVED** that the 2017 General Assembly encourages the Christian Church (Disciples of Christ) to expose and remove denominational structure which benefits from the Doctrine of Discovery; work toward eliminating the CDoD as a means to subjugate peoples, property, and land; develop resources for study; enter into self-examination; seek to recognize and understand the historical trauma of indigenous people and to recognize DOC's participation in the continuing effects of that trauma; and

(3) **BE IT FURTHER RESOLVED** that the 2017 General Assembly urges the Office of General Minister and President, National Convocation, Central Pastoral Office for Hispanic Ministries, North American Pacific/Asian Disciples, Global Ministries and Disciples Home Missions:[v], in consultation with Yakama Christian Mission's Advocate for Indigenous Justice, Reconciliation Ministry, and the Moderator(s) of ad hoc Landscape Mending Council to learn where their organization/entity/structure have benefited from the CDoD and assist Regions and Congregations in documenting and explaining the effects of the CDoD in the life of the Church; and

(4) **BE IT FURTHER RESOLVED** that the 2017 General Assembly encourage the leaders of the church's racial/ethnic constituencies to insist on an indigenous voice in all General Church and Office of General Minister and President meetings/conferences/etc., where leaders of the ethnic constituencies are invited; and

(5) **BE IT FURTHER RESOLVED** that the 2017 General Assembly encourages the church's educational affiliates (e.g., Colleges, Universities, Seminaries) to educate students on the Christian Doctrine of Discovery, how

the CDoD influenced past and current DOC polity and theology, support instructors to research and write on how the Christian Doctrine of Discovery has benefited and/or damaged their area of expertise and recruit and provide scholarships to Native people; and

(6) **BE IT FURTHER RESOLVED** that the 2017 General Assembly urges all Regions and congregations to develop and nurture relationships with the American Indian, Alaska Natives, or First Nation people of the place where they reside; and

(7) **FINALLY, BE IT RESOLVED** that the 2017 General Assembly encourages congregations to act and urge their State to offer a free curriculum about the history, culture, and government of federally recognized Indian Tribes within State boundaries to State school districts, and require districts to incorporate the curricula of their nearest Tribe(s) into their schools' curriculum [vi].

Notes:

[i] Find educational information on the Doctrine of Discovery at Yakama Christian Mission, http://wp.me/P6DjFC-2j.

[ii] US incarceration rates for American Indians (https://www.bjs.gov/content/pub/pdf/aic.pdfand https://www.prisonpolicy.org/graphs/2010percent/US_American_Indian_2010.html, suicide among American Indian/Alaska Native adolescents and young adults ages 15 to 34 is 1.5 times higher than the national average (https://www.cdc.gov/ViolencePrevention/pdf/Suicide-DataSheet-a.pdf), American Indian students are disproportionately disciplined (https://archive.unews.utah.edu/news_releases/american-indians-disproportionately-disciplined-at-school-compared-to-white-students-new-university-of-utah-research-shows/).

[iii] GA 1323: Incarceration, Justice and Restoration in the United States; GA 1324: Reflection on Christian Theology and Polity, the Christian Doctrine of Discovery, and the Indigenous Voice; GA 1518: Black Lives Matter: A Movement for All; GA 1519: Commemorating 100 Years Since the Armenian Genocide; GA 1520: Concerning Environmental Racism; 0313 Ending Violence Against Women—an essay on Native Human Trafficking can be found at: https://indiancountrymedianetwork.com/news/politics/trafficking-in-native-communities/.

[iv] Episcopal Church, Unitarian Universalist Association, United Church of Christ, New England Yearly Meeting-of Friends-Quakers, United Methodist Church, Anglican Church, Presbyterian Church (U.S.A.), World Council of Churches.

[v] Refugee & Immigration Ministries, Green Chalice, Disciples Women, and Disciples Men, Disciples of Christ Historical Society, Week of Compassion, National Benevolent Association, Pension Fund, Hope Partnership, Higher Education and Leadership Ministries, Disciples Church Extension Fund, Council on Christian Unity, Christian Church Foundation, Christian Board of Publication, College of Regional Ministers, Disciples Center for Public Witness, Disciples Peace Fellowship, European Evangelistic Society, National City Christian Church Foundation, and the United Christian Missionary Society.

[vi] Washington State adopted such an amendment, RCW 28A.320.170, which can be found at http://app.leg.wa.gov/Rcw/default.aspx?cite=28A.320.170.

QUESTIONS FOR REFLECTION:

1. What do you believe is the significance of this action by this church body?

2. What do you think could be the impact of such a statement?

3. What questions or concerns does this raise for you as it relates to the current challenges of immigration in America today?

Appendix F

American Attitudes Toward Immigration

(Public Religious Research Institute)

This research document is reprinted with the permission of the Public Religious Research Institute, Robert Jones, president.

Are Immigrants a Threat? Most Americans Don't Think So, but Those Receptive to the "Threat" Narrative Are Predictably More Anti-Immigrant

Introduction

Joe Biden campaigned on a commitment to reverse many of the Trump administration's strictest anti-immigration policies. Though many of these policies have either been reversed or halted—including the travel ban for people from various countries, the ban on temporary work visas, and the expansion of the public charge rule, among others—some remain in place.[1] One such policy is a public health rule known as Title 42, which allows for the immediate expulsion of migrants at the border in order to control the spread of COVID-19. The rule was set to be lifted in late December, but its suspension was delayed by the Supreme Court owing to public backlash and fears that illegal border crossings would increase significantly.[2]

Meanwhile, independent Sen. Kyrsten Sinema and Republican Sen. Thom Tillis have proposed legislation that would both extend Title 42 and provide a pathway to citizenship for two million people who were illegally brought to the United States as children and are now classified as "Dreamers." The proposal also includes new resources to speed the processing of asylum seekers.[3]

As politicians struggle with how to address immigration issues, Americans' views on immigration have become increasingly polarized, with Republicans becoming significantly more anti-immigrant in their attitudes over the past few years. Republicans have continually attacked the Biden administration's handling of immigration, claiming that his policies will increase the flow of immigrants over the southern border and calling for U.S. Secretary of Homeland Security Alejandro Mayorkas to resign. These criticisms are expected to increase now that Republicans have regained control of the House of Representatives.[4]

Though the Trump-era narrative still resonates among certain portions of the American public, this report reveals that majorities of Americans do not view immigrants as a threat. But people who are more likely to think of immigrants as a threat—including those who most trust conservative media sources and Fox News—they are considerably more anti-immigrant and less supportive of open immigration policies.

Immigrants as a Threat to Traditional American Customs and Values

A majority of Americans (55%) say the growing number of newcomers from other countries strengthens American society, while four in ten (40%) say the growing number of newcomers from other countries threatens traditional American customs and values. Republicans (69%) are about twice as likely as independents (37%) and about four more times as likely as Democrats (17%) to say newcomers threaten traditional American customs and values. Though there is now a 52-percentage-point difference between Republicans and Democrats on this question, a little over a decade ago, in 2011, the difference was much lower, at 22 percentage points (Republicans 55% vs. Democrats 33%).

Among religious groups surveyed, white Christians are the most likely to think that newcomers threaten traditional American customs and values. This includes about two-thirds of white evangelical Protestants (65%), a slim majority of white mainline Protestants (53%) and half of white Catholics (50%). By contrast, four in ten other Christians (40%) and about three in ten Hispanic Catholics (31%), Black Protestants (29%), religiously unaffiliated Americans (27%), and members of non-Christian religions (27%) also say immigrants are a threat to American society.[5]

White Americans (46%) are notably more likely than Hispanic Americans (31%), Americans of another race (31%), and Black Americans (28%) to think that newcomers threaten traditional American customs and values.[6] Furthermore, white Americans without a four-year college degree are notably more likely than those with a four-year college degree to hold this view (53% vs. 34%).

People's views on this topic are significantly affected by whether they know people who are immigrants or are immigrants themselves. Documented immigrants and those who know someone who is a documented immigrant are less likely than those who do not know any documented immigrants to say newcomers threaten traditional American customs and values (36% vs. 49%). The same is true for those who do and don't know any undocumented immigrants (33% vs. 43%).

Americans' proximity to people of different races and ethnicities also has an impact on whether they think immigrants threaten American customs and values. About four in ten Americans who are close friends with or know someone of a different race (39%) say that immigrants threaten traditional American customs and values, compared with a slim majority of those who don't know anyone of a different race or ethnicity (51%).

Answers to the threat question also correlate with media consumption. Those who most trust conservative television media (76%) or Fox News (74%) are significantly more likely than those whose most trusted news source is a non-television source (42%) or a mainstream television source (28%) to say that newcomers from other countries threaten traditional American customs and values.

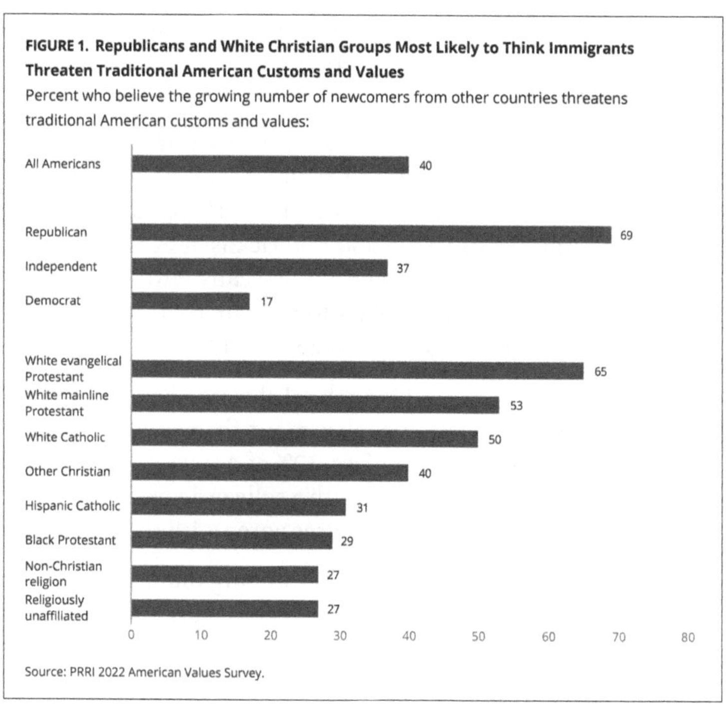

Belief in Cultural Replacement Theory

The "great replacement" theory—a conspiracy theory touted by white supremacists that claims nonwhite people are invading or immigrating to the United States in order to push white voters and citizens into the minority—appears to be becoming more mainstream among the political right. While most Americans do not agree with replacement theory, a key minority do. Three in ten Americans (30%) completely or mostly agree with the statement "immigrants are invading our country and replacing our cultural and ethnic background," while nearly two-thirds (64%) completely or mostly disagree. Republicans (55%) are the outliers, as they are more than four times as likely as Democrats (12%) and twice as likely as independents (27%) to agree.

White Christian subgroups exhibit the most support for replacement theory: half of white evangelical Protestants (51%) and 41% of both white mainline Protestants and white Catholics agree that immigrants are invading the country. In contrast, 26% of members of other Christian religions, 21% of members of non-

Christian religions, 21% of religiously unaffiliated Americans, 19% of Black Protestants, and 19% of Hispanic Catholics agree with this statement.

Among racial groups, white Americans remain the most likely to agree with this cultural replacement statement, with 36% agreeing, compared to about one-fifth of Hispanic Americans (21%), Black Americans (19%), and Americans of other races and ethnicities (22%). However, white Americans with a four-year college degree are notably less likely to agree than white Americans without a four-year college degree (26% vs. 43%).

Across demographics, a higher level of education is associated with lower agreement with replacement theory: 37% of those with a high school education or less, 30% of Americans with some college experience, 25% of those with a college degree, and 19% of Americans with a postgraduate degree agree with the statement.

Meanwhile, agreement is higher among older age groups: 19% of Americans ages 18–29, 25% of those ages 30–49, 35% of those ages 50–64, and 43% of those age 65 and older agree that immigrants are invading our country and replacing our cultural and ethnic background.

Whether people personally know any immigrants has a substantial impact on attitudes toward replacement theory. Only about one in four Americans who are or know someone who is a documented immigrant (27%) or who are or know someone who is an undocumented immigrant (26%) agree with replacement theory. However, 38% of those who do not know anyone who is a documented immigrant and 33% of those who do not know any undocumented immigrants agree.

Partisan differences are still present, however. A slim majority of Republicans who know a documented immigrant (51%) or an undocumented immigrant (54%) agree that immigrants are invading the country, compared with 64% of Republicans who do not know any documented immigrants and 57% of those who do not know any undocumented immigrants. By contrast, Democrats are notably less likely to agree with replacement theory, regardless of whether they know any documented (9%) or undocumented immigrants (11%) or do not know anyone who is a documented (18%) or undocumented immigrant (13%).

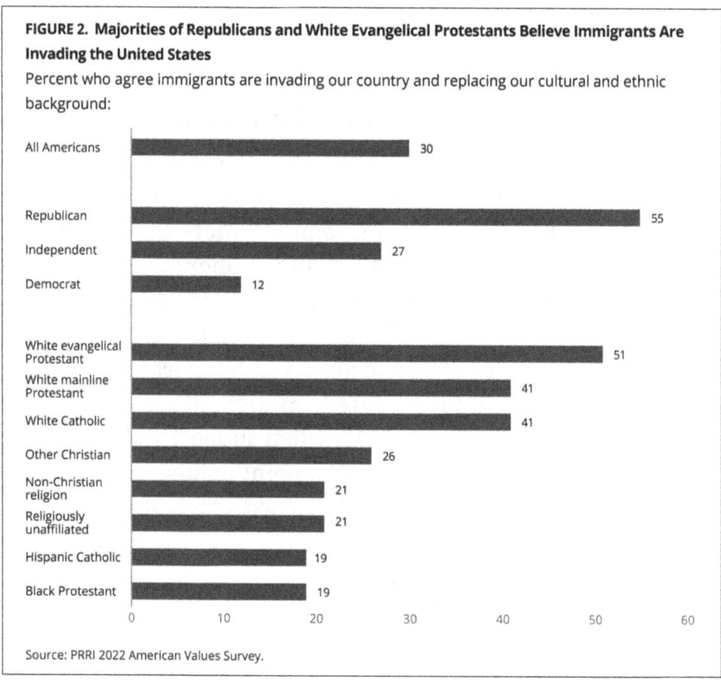

A majority of Americans who most trust conservative media outlets (70%) and Fox News (56%) among television news sources believe immigrants are invading our country and replacing our cultural and ethnic background, compared with 31% of those whose most trusted news source is a non-television source and 21% who most trust a mainstream television source.

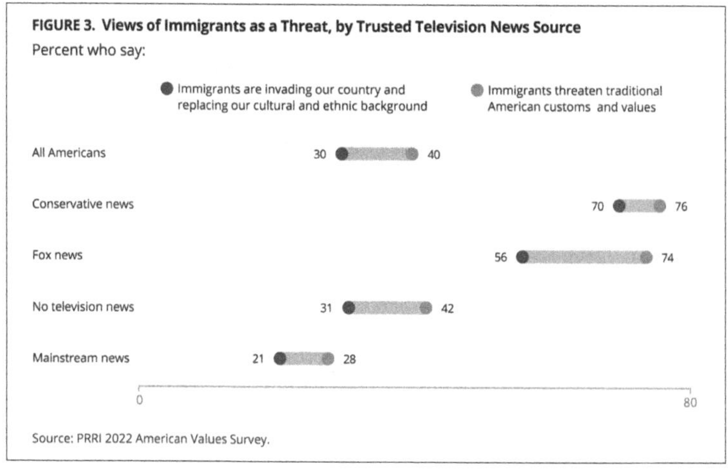

Immigration Policies

Support for Pathway to Citizenship for All Undocumented Immigrants and for Dreamers

Nearly six in ten Americans (57%) say that immigrants living in the United States illegally should be given a way to become citizens, provided they meet certain requirements. More than one in ten (13%) say they would prefer that undocumented immigrants be eligible for permanent residency status but not citizenship, and one in four (25%) say all immigrants living in the country illegally should be identified and deported. Support for a pathway to citizenship for undocumented immigrants has remained remarkably consistent since 2013, when support was at 63%. In those years, support was at its lowest point in July of 2014 at 58% and September of 2022 at 57% and reached a high of 67% in 2019.

Support is lower for a pathway to citizenship for "Dreamers," children brought illegally to the United States by their parents who are eligible for temporary legal status, but have to renew their status every two years. When informed of the current policy, 41% of Americans say the policy should be changed to allow children of undocumented immigrants to apply for citizenship or permanent resident status. About one-third of respondents (32%) say the policy should be left as it is, and about one in five (22%) say those brought to the country illegally as children should be identified and deported.[7]

Democrats have become more supportive of a path to citizenship for undocumented immigrants in recent years, with support increasing from 71% in 2013, when PRRI first asked the question, to 77% today. By contrast, Republicans (40%) are less supportive in 2022 than they were in 2013 (53%). Today, 10% of Republicans say they would prefer for undocumented immigrants to be eligible for permanent residency status but not citizenship, and nearly half (48%) say all immigrants living in the U.S. illegally should be deported—an increase from 44% in 2021 and 32% in 2013.

When it comes to Dreamers, Democrats (66%) are more than three times as likely as Republicans (18%) to support a pathway to citizenship or permanent residency. Meanwhile, 37% of

Republicans and 28% of Democrats say the policy should be left as it is. Just 5% of Democrats say that Dreamers should be identified and deported, compared with more than four in ten Republicans (43%). Independents closely resemble all Americans on this issue, with a 42% plurality supporting a pathway to citizenship or permanent residency for Dreamers, 35% supporting the program as it is, and 19% supporting deportation.

Religious Tradition

Majorities of almost all religious groups support allowing undocumented immigrants to become citizens, including 73% of Black Protestants, 66% of religiously unaffiliated Americans, 62% of Hispanic Catholics, 60% of members of non-Christian religions, 58% of other Christians, 54% of white mainline Protestants, and 54% of white Catholics. White evangelical Protestants stand out as the only religious group in which a majority does not support a path to citizenship for undocumented immigrants, with only 42% expressing support. White evangelical Protestants are also the most likely to say undocumented immigrants should be identified and deported, with 49% expressing this view.

By contrast, the only religious groups in which majorities support a pathway to citizenship or residence for Dreamers are Black Protestants (57%), Hispanic Catholics (55%), and religiously unaffiliated Americans (54%). By contrast, only 42% of other Christians, 40% of members of non-Christian religions, 35% of white mainline Protestants, and 30% of white Catholics support this policy change. White evangelical Protestants are the least likely to support giving Dreamers a pathway to citizenship (21%) and the most likely to say that undocumented children of immigrants should be identified and deported (40%).

Demographics

Majorities of every racial and ethnic group support a pathway to citizenship for undocumented immigrants, including 53% of other races, 55% of white Americans, 64% of Black Americans, and 64% of Hispanic Americans. Among white Americans, those with a college degree are more likely to support this policy than those who do not have a college degree (61% vs. 51%). On the question of giving Dreamers a pathway to citizenship or permanent residency, slim majorities of Black Americans (53%) and Hispanic Americans (52%) express support, as do more than one-third of white Americans (37%) and Americans of other races (36%). White Americans with a college degree are notably more likely to support this policy than whites without a college degree (46% vs. 32%).

Majorities of Americans across all age groups support a pathway to citizenship for all undocumented immigrants, including 65% of Americans ages 18–29, 56% of Americans ages 30–49), 57% of Americans ages 50–64, and 54% of Americans 65 and over. However, Americans of ages 18–29 (54%) are the only group in which a majority supports a pathway to citizenship or permanent residency for Dreamers. This policy doesn't reach majority support among any of the other age groups: ages 30–40 (45%), ages 50–64 (33%), age 65 years and over (34%).

Support for a pathway to citizenship for all undocumented immigrants is higher among women (60%) than among men (55%). The same is true of support for a pathway for Dreamers, though support is lower on this question among both women (45%) and men (38%).

Perceptions of Threat

Nearly four in ten Americans who think that immigrants are a threat to traditional American values and customs (38%) also say that undocumented immigrants should be allowed a way to become citizens provided they meet certain requirements, and one in ten (11%) say they should be allowed to become permanent legal residents but not citizens. Half of Americans who view immigrants as a threat (50%) say that undocumented immigrants should be identified and deported. This number rises to 58% among Republicans who view immigrants as a threat, while only about 24% of Democrats in this group think the same.

Among Americans who think immigrants are invading the country and replacing our cultural and ethnic background, 33% say that undocumented immigrants should be allowed a way to become citizens if they meet certain requirements, and 10% say they should be allowed to become permanent legal residents but not citizens. A majority of this group (56%) say undocumented immigrants should be identified and deported, with Republicans (62%) more than twice as likely as Democrats (28%) to agree with this statement.

These patterns hold for Dreamers. Only 18% of those who think immigrants are a threat say that Dreamers should be allowed to apply for citizenship or permanent residency. But 35% of this group say the current policy should be left as it is and 45% say that Dreamers should be identified and deported—a view that is supported by 55% of Republicans in this group and 19% of Democrats.

Among those who think immigrants are invading the country and replacing its cultural and ethnic background, 15% say the policy should be changed to allow Dreamers to apply for citizenship or permanent residency, 33% say the policy should be left as it is, and a slim majority (51%) say Dreamers should be identified and deported. This last number jumps to 59% among Republicans in this group, compared to 23% of Democrats.

FIGURE 4. Most Republicans Who Think of Immigrants as a Threat Support Deportation of Undocumented Immigrants and Dreamers

Percent who say:

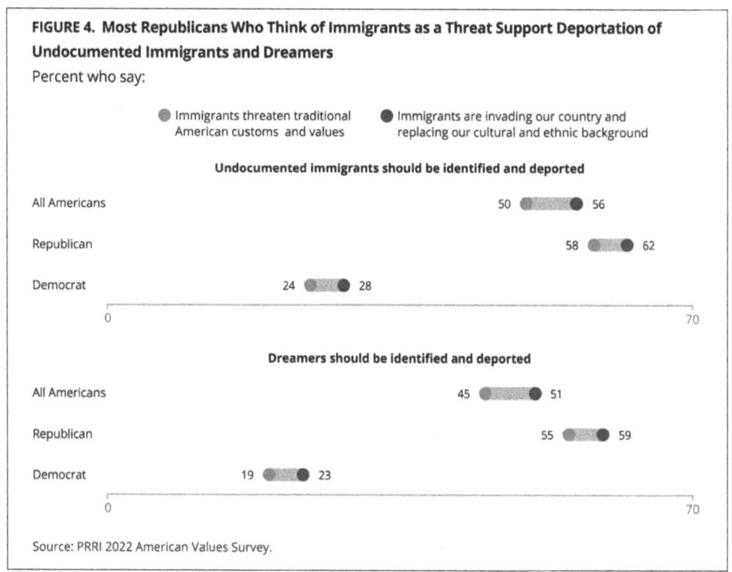

Source: PRRI 2022 American Values Survey.

Media Consumption

Support for these policies also varies according to which news sources respondents said they most trusted. Those who most trust conservative media outlets (22%) and Fox News (38%) among television news sources are less likely than those who most trust a non-television source (54%) or a mainstream television source (70%) to support a pathway to citizenship for undocumented immigrants. However, Americans are notably less supportive of Dreamers across all of these media-consumption groups (12%, 13%, 40%, and 53%, respectively). In fact, majorities of Americans who most trust conservative television news sources say undocumented immigrants (67%) and Dreamers (62%) should be identified and deported, compared to 46% and 43%, respectively among those who trust Fox News. Three in ten or fewer of those who do not trust a television news source or trust mainstream news support identifying and deporting immigrants and Dreamers.

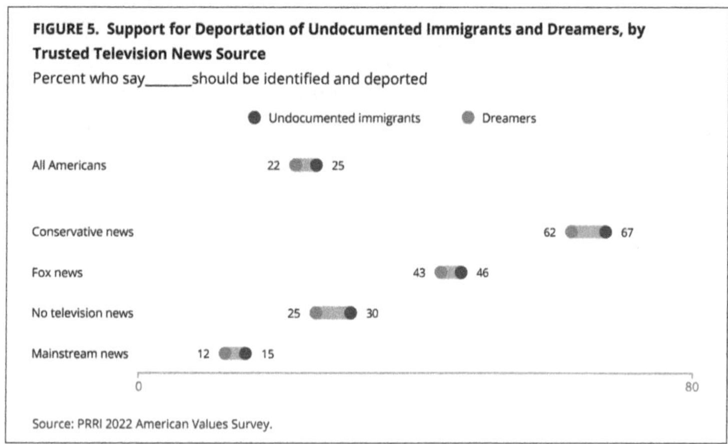

Support for Refugees and Work Immigrants

Accepting Afghan Refugees vs. Ukrainian Refugees

With the United States pulling its troops out of Afghanistan in 2021 and the conflict between Ukraine and Russia escalating in early 2022, PRRI asked Americans if they favor or oppose accepting more refugees from these two nations into the U.S. The results showed stark differences: a majority of Americans (60%) favor accepting more refugees from Ukraine, compared to 45% who favor accepting more refugees from Afghanistan. These differences are evident across party affiliation and every demographic group.

Even though Republicans are less likely than Democrats to favor accepting refugees overall, they are significantly less likely to favor accepting more Afghan refugees (26%) than they are Ukrainian refugees (48%). A majority of Democrats favor accepting more refugees from Afghanistan (65%) but even more favor accepting Ukrainian refugees (78%). Independents mirror all Americans.

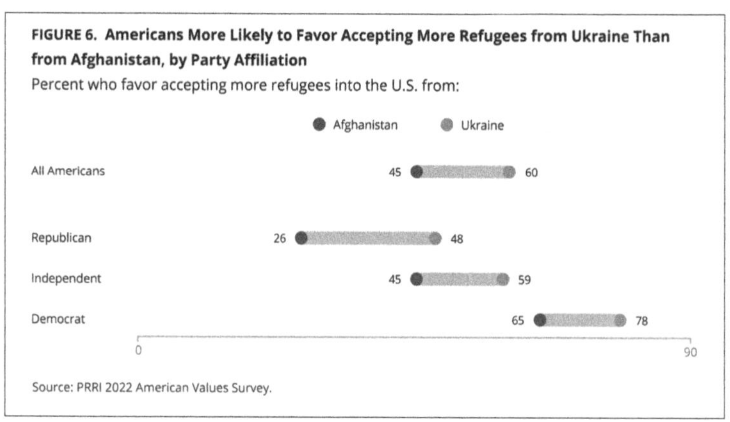

FIGURE 6. Americans More Likely to Favor Accepting More Refugees from Ukraine Than from Afghanistan, by Party Affiliation
Percent who favor accepting more refugees into the U.S. from:

Source: PRRI 2022 American Values Survey.

Majorities across all religious groups favor accepting more refugees from Ukraine, including 70% of White Catholics, 66% of Hispanic Catholics, 64% of white mainline Protestants, 64% of members of non-Christian religions, 62% of religiously unaffiliated Americans, 56% of Black Protestants and other Christians, and 48% of white evangelical Protestants. However, Hispanic Catholics (55%) and religiously unaffiliated Americans (54%) are the only groups in which a majority favor accepting more refugees from Afghanistan. Less than half of white Catholics (47%), 43% of Black Protestants, 42% of other Christians, 41% of white mainline Protestants, 39% of members of non-Christian religions, and only 31% of white evangelical Protestants favor accepting more refugees from Afghanistan.

Across racial groups, a similar pattern emerges in which Americans are more willing to accept more Ukrainian refugees than to accept more Afghan refugees. This is true among white Americans (62% vs. 45%), Hispanic Americans (63% vs. 48%), other-race Americans (56% vs. 38%), and Black Americans (50% vs.

40%). However, whites with a college degree are more accepting of both Ukrainian (76%) and Afghan refugees (61%) than are whites without a college degree (52% and 36%, respectively).

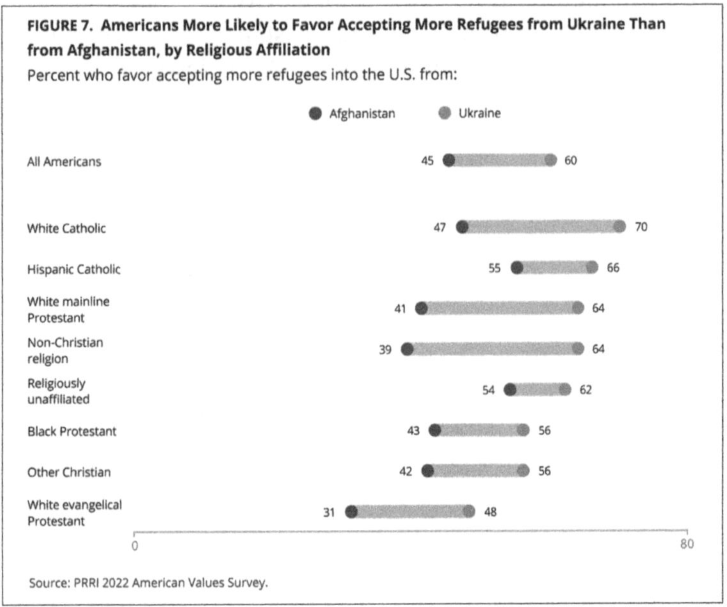

Not surprisingly, Americans who think that immigrants pose a threat to traditional values and customs are notably less likely than all Americans to favor accepting more refugees from Ukraine, with 44% expressing support, but this number is even smaller when it comes to refugees from Afghanistan, at only 18%. Similarly, Americans who think that immigrants are invading our country and replacing our ethnic and cultural background are notably less likely to favor accepting more refugees from Ukraine (43%) and even less likely to favor accepting those from Afghanistan (15%).

Americans who most trust Fox News among television news sources are the least likely to favor accepting more refugees from both Ukraine (47%) and Afghanistan (23%), compared with those whose most trusted news source is a non-television source (53% and 41%, respectively) or a mainstream television source (74% and 56%).[8]

Accepting Highly Skilled vs. Low-Skilled Immigrants

Americans are significantly more likely to favor accepting more highly skilled immigrants (69%) into the United States than to favor accepting more low-skilled immigrants (39%), and this is true across all party affiliations and demographic groups. In fact, across demographics, there is not much variation in support for accepting more highly skilled immigrants into the country, and majorities of Republicans (58%), independents (75%), and Democrats (80%) all express support.

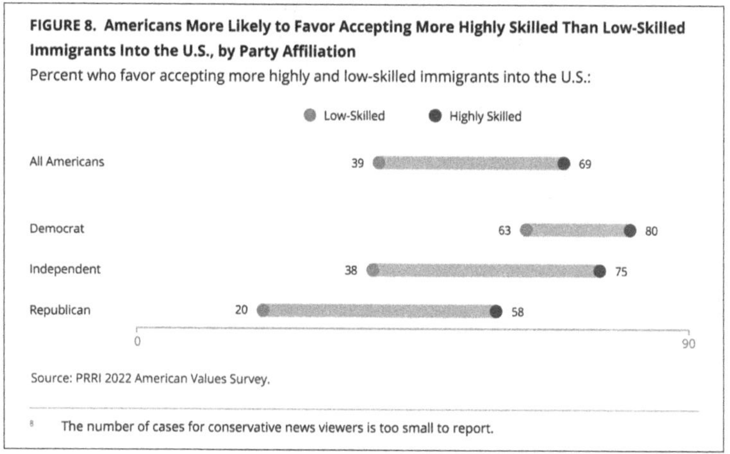

Similarly, 57% of white evangelical Protestants, 63% of other Christians, two-thirds of Black Protestants (65%) and white mainline Protestants (66%), 72% of white Catholics, 75% of religiously unaffiliated Americans, 82% of Hispanic Catholics, and 89% of members of non-Christian religions favor accepting more highly skilled immigrants into the country.

By contrast, only 20% of Republicans are in favor of accepting more low-skilled immigrants into the United States, compared with 38% of independents and 63% of Democrats.

Religiously unaffiliated Americans (51%) and members of non-Christian religions (59%) are the only two religious groups in which majorities favor accepting more low-skilled immigrants. A minority of all other groups express support, including 47% of Black Protestants, 41% of Hispanic Catholics, 34% of both white mainline Protestants and white Catholics, 31% of white Catholics, and 25% of white evangelical Protestants.

At least half the members of every racial group are supportive of accepting more high-skilled immigrants, including 63% of Hispanic Americans, 62% of white Americans, 56% of Americans of other races, and 50% of Black Americans. However, Americans of every racial group are notably less likely to accept low-skilled immigrants, including 48% of Hispanic Americans, 45% of white Americans, 38% of Americans of other races, and 40% of Black Americans. White Americans with a college degree are notably more supportive of accepting both highly skilled (76%) and low-skilled (61%) immigrants than are whites without a college degree (52% and 36%, respectively).

FIGURE 9. Americans More Likely to Favor Accepting More Highly Skilled Than Low-Skilled Immigrants Into the U.S., by Religious Affiliation

Percent who favor accepting more highly and low-skilled immigrants into the U.S.:

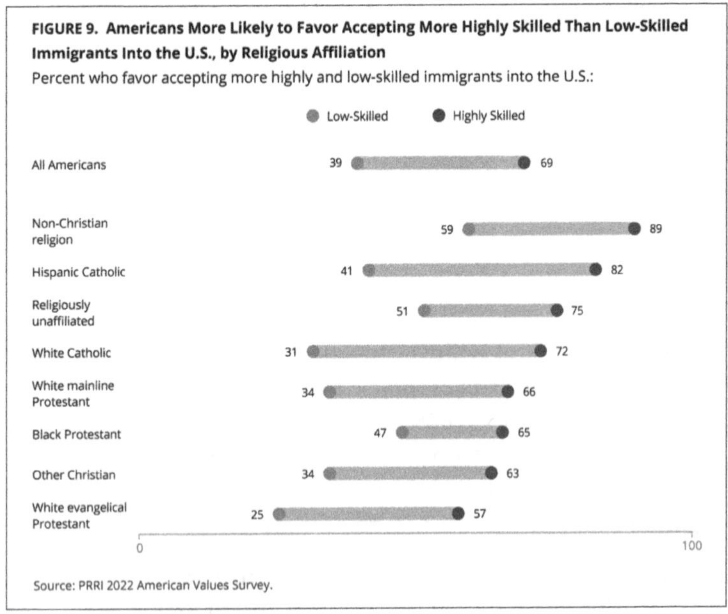

Source: PRRI 2022 American Values Survey.

Interestingly, even among Americans who view immigrants as a threat to traditional values and customs, a majority (52%) favor accepting high-skilled immigrants into the United States, though only 14% support accepting low-skilled immigrants. A similar pattern emerges among Americans who think that immigrants are invading our country and replacing our ethnic and cultural background: about half (48%) favor accepting high-skilled immigrants into the United States, while only 15% favor accepting low-skilled immigrants.

Across media-consumption groups, solid majorities favor accepting high-skilled immigrants, including 74% of those who most trust a mainstream television source, 69% of those who most trust a non-television source, and 67% of those who most trust Fox News. By contrast, 49% of those who most trust a mainstream television source, 38% of those who trust non-television sources, and only 18% of those who trust Fox News favor accepting low-skilled immigrants.[9]

Accepting More Immigrants Based on What Types of Jobs Are Available

Americans are divided on the question of accepting more immigrants into the United States based on what types of jobs are available, with 53% favoring and 43% opposing the idea, and there is considerable variation across different groups.

About two-thirds of Democrats (65%), 56% of independents, and 41% of Republicans favor accepting more immigrants based on the jobs available.

Hispanic Catholics (76%) are the most likely to favor this policy, followed by members of non-Christian religions (67%), religiously unaffiliated Americans (58%), and other Christians (53%). About half of white Catholics (51%), white mainline Protestants (50%), and Black Protestants (49%) also favor this policy, compared with only 38% of white evangelicals.

Black Americans (43%) are the least likely to favor accepting immigrants based on the types of jobs available, compared with 50% of white Americans, 60% of other-race Americans, and 66% of Hispanics. Whites with a college degree are more likely to favor this policy than are whites without a college degree (64% vs. 42%).

Support for this policy generally increases with education: 45% of Americans with a high school degree or less, 50% of Americans with some college, 65% of Americans with a college degree, and 64% of Americans with a postgraduate degree express support.

By contrast, support decreases with age: 57% of Americans ages 18–29, 54% of Americans ages 30–49, 49% of Americans 50–64, and 51% of Americans 65 or over support the policy. Men are more likely than women to favor accepting immigrants based on the types of jobs available (56% vs. 49%).

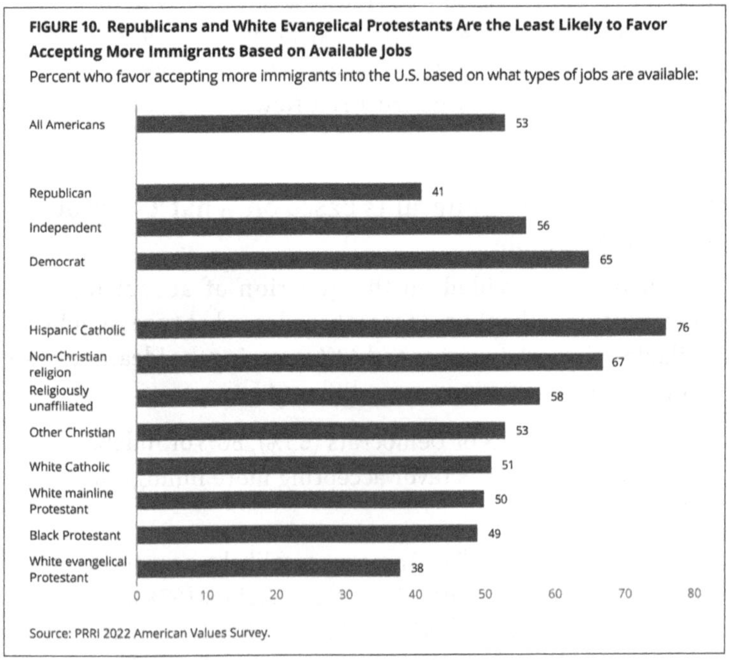

Among Americans who think that immigrants are a threat to traditional values and customs, 38% favor accepting more immigrants into the United States based on what jobs are available. The level of support is about the same as among those who think that immigrants are invading the country and replacing its ethnic and cultural background (36%).

Americans who most trust Fox News (49%) or a non-television source (50%) are less likely than those who most trust a mainstream television source (60%) to favor accepting more immigrants into the U.S. based on the types of jobs available.

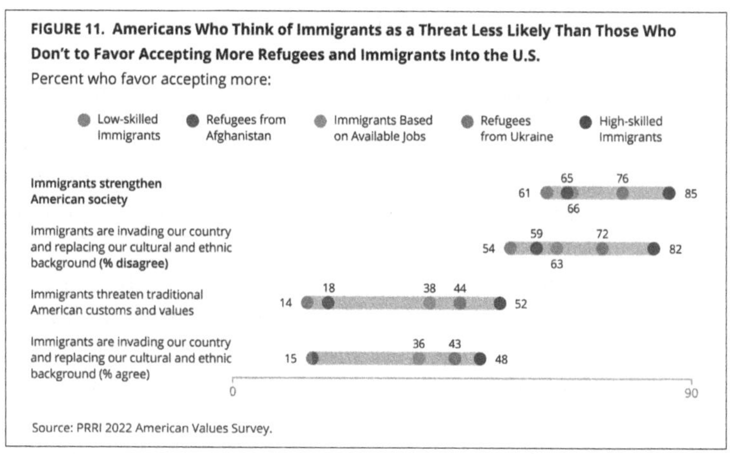

FIGURE 11. Americans Who Think of Immigrants as a Threat Less Likely Than Those Who Don't to Favor Accepting More Refugees and Immigrants Into the U.S.

Source: PRRI 2022 American Values Survey.

General Views About the Country and Views of Immigrants as a Threat

Views About the Country and Immigrants as a Threat to Traditional Customs and Values

Among Americans who say things in this country are going in the right direction, only 17% say that immigrants are threatening traditional American values and customs, compared with 48% of those who say that the country is going in the wrong direction. The partisan divide remains, though: Republicans who say that the country is going in the wrong direction are about three times more likely than Democrats in that group to think that immigrants are threatening American society (72% vs. 23%).

The majority of those who say America's culture and way of life have mostly changed for the worse since the 1950s (56%) also believe that the growing number of newcomers threatens traditional American customs and values, compared with only 24% of those who think the country has mostly changed for the better. Negative views of immigrants are higher among Republicans who think that American culture and way of life has changed for the worse (74%) than among Republicans who think it has changed for the better (60%). There is a similar difference among Democrats, though Democrats are generally less likely to hold negative views of immigrants. Democrats who think that American society has changed for the worse (32%) are about three times more likely than Democrats who think it has changed for the better (11%) to say that immigrants are a threat to American customs and values.

Of those who view President Joe Biden favorably, only 17% say that newcomers are a threat to American customs and values. This is in stark contrast to those who view him unfavorably, among whom a majority (58%) think immigrants are a threat. Viewing immigrants as a threat to American customs and values is even less common among Americans who strongly approve of Biden as president (16%), or among those who approve of Biden's handling of immigration (14%). By contrast, among those who view former President Donald Trump favorably, the vast majority (71%) say that newcomers are threatening American society, compared with 24% of those who view Trump unfavorably.

Florida Gov. Ron DeSantis has recently come to the forefront of national politics, partly because of policies that involve taking a tough stand on immigration issues. Unsurprisingly, Americans who view DeSantis favorably are notably more likely than those who view him unfavorably to say that newcomers are a threat to American customs and values (69% vs. 22%).

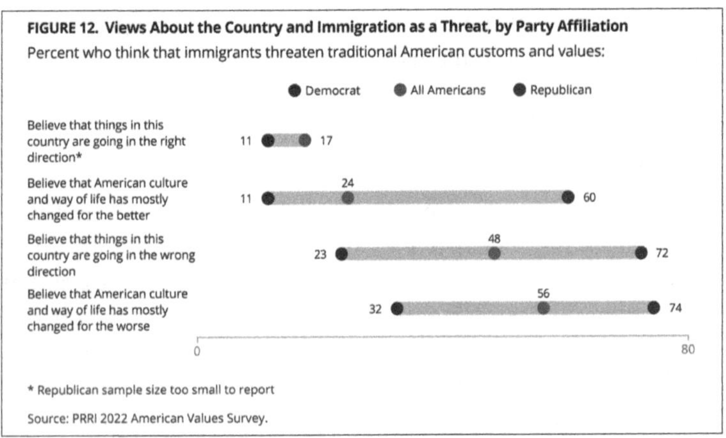

Critical Issues and Views of Immigrants as a Threat to Traditional Customs and Values

Four in ten Americans (40%) say that immigration was a critical issue in deciding how they vote in the 2022 midterm elections.

Among this group, 63% view newcomers as threatening American customs and values, while 35% think immigrants strengthen the country. Republicans in this group are about three times as likely as Democrats to think immigrants threaten traditional American customs and values (78% vs. 25%)

Among the 47% of Americans who considered crime a critical issue in the midterm election, the majority (53%) think that immigrants threaten traditional American customs and values, compared with 44% who think immigrants strengthen the country. Republicans who find crime to be a critical issue are substantially more likely than Democrats who think the same to say that immigrants threaten traditional American customs and values (74% vs. 22%).

Among the one-third of Americans (33%) who considered jobs and unemployment to be a critical issue in the midterm election, their views of immigrants is divided: 50% see newcomers as a strength, and 48% see them as a threat to American society. Among Republicans in this group, 74% say that immigrants are a threat, compared with 17% of Democrats in this group.

FIGURE 13. Critical Issues for Midterm Voting and Views of Immigrants, by Party Affiliation
Percent who say that immigrants threaten traditional American customs and values among those who say the following issues are critical:

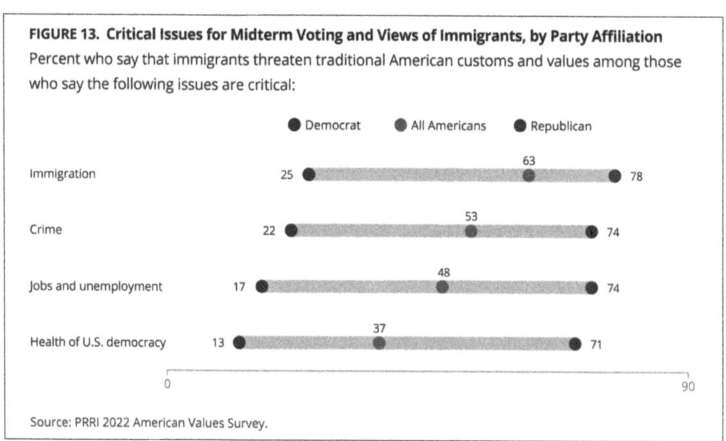

Source: PRRI 2022 American Values Survey.

Interestingly, among the 57% of Americans who considered the health of the country's democracy to be a critical election issue, there is a significant divide in views of immigrants: 37% think that immigrants are a threat to traditional American customs and values, including 71% of Republicans in this group and only

13% of Democrats, compared with 61% who think that immigrants strengthen the country.

Views About the Country, QAnon Beliefs, and Agreement with Replacement Theory

Americans who say that things in this country are going in the wrong direction are more than twice as likely as those who say things are going in the right direction to agree with replacement theory (36% vs. 14%). Of Republicans who state that things in this country are going in the wrong direction, 58% also say immigrants are invading the country and replacing our cultural and ethnic background. By contrast, among Democrats who believe the country is headed in the wrong direction, only 14% say this about immigrants.

Similarly, those who say that the American culture and way of life have changed for the worse since the 1950s are more likely to say that immigrants are invading the country than are those who say it has changed for the better (45% vs. 16%). Among people who say American culture has worsened, Republicans (61%) are three times as likely as Democrats (20%) to agree that immigrants are invading the country.

There is also a stark division that emerges with respect to favored politicians. Among those who view President Joe Biden favorably, only 14% agree that immigrants are replacing our country's culture and ethnic background. By contrast, majorities of those who have favorable views of former President Donald Trump (56%) and Florida Gov. Ron DeSantis (54%) agree with replacement theory.

Six in ten Americans who are QAnon believers (60%) agree with replacement theory, compared with about one-third of QAnon doubters (32%) and one in ten QAnon rejecters (11%).[10] Notably, nearly eight in ten Republicans who are QAnon believers (79%) also believe in replacement theory.[11]

A majority of those who believe that American life needs to be protected from foreign influence (56%) also believe that immigrants are invading our country and replacing our cultural and ethnic background. Unsurprisingly, there are substantial partisan differences: among those who believe that American life needs to be protected against foreign influence, roughly one-third of Democrats (34%) support replacement theory, compared with more than two-thirds of Republicans (69%).

The majority of Americans who agree that God intended America to be a new promised land for European Christians also agree with replacement theory, with 55% holding these views. Distinct partisan differences appear once again: 70% of Republicans who believe that God intended America to be a new promised land also view immigrants as an invading force, compared with 39% of Democrats.

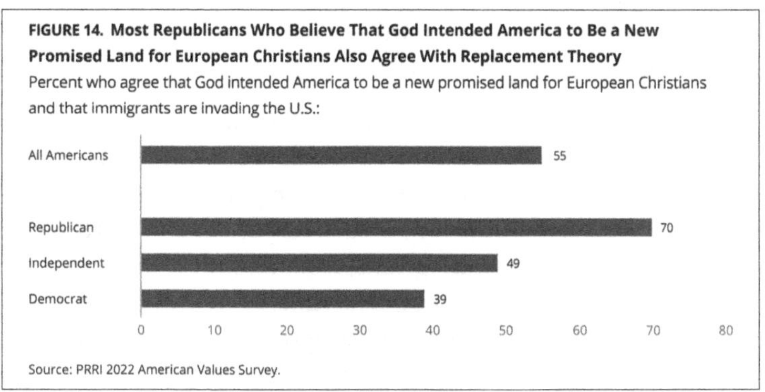

Critical Issues and Agreement with Replacement Theory

Of those who consider immigration to be a critical issue in the midterm election, a slim majority think immigrants are invading the country and replacing our cultural and ethnic background (53%). Republicans in this group (66%) are more than three times as likely as Democrats (20%) to agree.

Among Americans who think that crime is a critical issue in the midterm election, a plurality of 44% agree with replacement theory, including a majority of Republicans (63%) and just 17% of Democrats in this group.

Among Americans who consider jobs and unemployment to be a critical election issue, 38% agree with replacement theory, including 62% of Republicans and 15% of Democrats in this group.

An even larger divide is present among those who saw the health of the country's democracy as a critical issue in the midterm election. Three in ten in this group (31%) agree with replacement theory, and Republicans are six times as likely as Democrats to do so (60% vs. 10%).

Negative Attitudes toward Immigrants

When asked about their attitudes toward immigrants coming to the United States today, a majority of Americans say that immigrants make an effort to learn English (57% agree vs. 40% disagree), but they are divided on whether immigrants burden local communities by using more than their share of social services (46% agree vs. 51% disagree). Meanwhile, about one-third agree that immigrants increase crime in local communities (35% agree vs. 61% disagree) and that immigrants take jobs from Americans (34% vs. 62%).

With the exception of respondents' views of immigrants as making an effort to learn English, the responses to these questions correlate very strongly. Therefore, a four-point composite index was developed to measure where each respondent stands on their overall attitude toward immigrants, from very unfavorable to very favorable.[12] According to this index, Americans are almost evenly divided in their attitudes toward immigrants, with 51% exhibiting unfavorable attitudes and 49% expressing favorable ones. This includes 17% who show very unfavorable attitudes and 15% who show very favorable attitudes.

Most Republicans (79%) hold negative views of immigrants, compared with 48% of independents and 28% of Democrats.

Majorities of several Christian groups hold negative attitudes toward immigrants, including 73% of white evangelical Protestants, 62% of both white mainline Protestants and white Catholics, and 58% of other Christians. Less than half of both Black Protestants (43%) and members of non-Christian religions (43%), along with about one-third of the religiously unaffiliated (36%) and Hispanic Catholics (33%), also hold negative attitudes.

A majority of white Americans (57%) hold negative views of immigrants, compared with 49% of other-race Americans, 41% of Hispanics, and 39% of Black Americans. However, white

Americans with a college degree hold views that are notably less negative than those of whites without a college degree (45% vs. 64%). Men are more likely than women to hold negative views of immigrants (55% vs. 47%), and younger Americans are less likely to do so than older Americans. Among those ages 18–29, 43% hold negative views, as do 45% of those ages 30–49, and 58% of both people ages 50–64 and those age 65 and older.

Among Americans who think that immigrants are a threat to traditional values and customs, the vast majority hold negative views of immigrants (84%) and the same is true among those who say that immigrants are invading the country and replacing its ethnic and cultural background (86%).

Negative attitudes toward immigrants also correlate with media consumption. The overwhelming majority of those who most trust conservative media (90%) and Fox News (84%) among television news sources hold negative views toward immigrants, compared with a slim majority of those who most trust a non-television source (52%) and about four in ten of those who trust a mainstream television source (39%).

FIGURE 15. Republicans and White Christian Groups Are the Most Likely to Hold Negative Views Toward Immigrants

Combined scale of negative views toward immigrants:

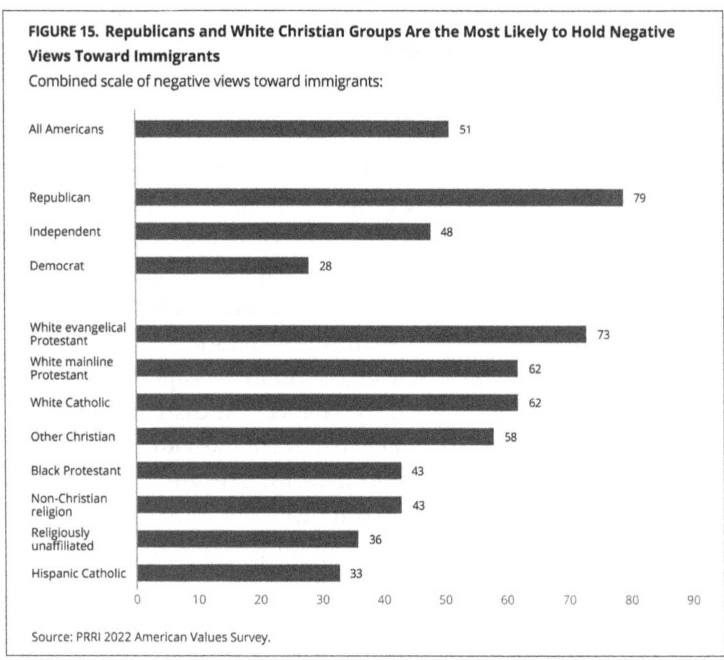

Source: PRRI 2022 American Values Survey.

Survey Methodology

The survey was designed and conducted by PRRI. The survey was made possible through the generous support of the Carnegie Corporation of New York, with additional support from the Ford Foundation and the Unitarian Universalist Veatch Program at Shelter Rock. The survey was conducted among a representative sample of 2,523 adults (age 18 and up) living in all 50 states in the United States, who are part of Ipsos's Knowledge Panel. Interviews were conducted online between September 1–11, 2022.

Respondents are recruited to the Knowledge Panel using an address-based sampling methodology from the Delivery Sequence File of the USPS—a database with full coverage of all delivery addresses in the U.S. As such, it covers all households regardless of their phone status, providing a representative online sample. Unlike opt-in panels, households are not permitted to "self-select" into the panel; and are generally limited [in] how many surveys they can take within a given time period.

The initial sample drawn from the Knowledge Panel was adjusted using pre-stratification weights so that it approximates the adult US population defined by the latest March supplement of the Current Population Survey. Next, a probability proportional to size (PPS) sampling scheme was used to select a representative sample.

To reduce the effects of any non-response bias, a post-stratification adjustment was applied based on demographic distributions from the most recent American Community Survey (ACS). The post-stratification weight rebalanced the sample based on the following benchmarks: age, race and ethnicity, gender, Census division, metro area, education, and income. The sample weighting was accomplished using an iterative proportional fitting (IFP) process that simultaneously balances the distributions of all variables. Weights were trimmed to prevent individual interviews from having too much influence on the final results. In addition to an overall national weight, separate weights were computed for each state to ensure that the demographic characteristics of the sample closely approximate the demographic characteristics of the target populations. The state-level post-stratification weights rebalanced the sample based on the following benchmarks: age, race and ethnicity, gender, education, and income.

The margin of error for the national survey is +/- 2.3 percentage points at the 95% level of confidence, including the design effect for the survey of 1.35. In addition to sampling error, surveys may also be subject to error or bias due to question wording, context, and order effects. Additional details about the Knowledge Panel can be found on the Ipsos website: https://www.ipsos.com/en-us/solution/knowledgepanel.

Endnotes

[1] The public charge rule was a policy that denied a green card, visa, or admission into the United States to any person likely to become dependent on government benefits. https://www.uscis.gov/public-charge

[2] https://www.nytimes.com/2022/12/29/us/title-42-border-el-paso.html?searchResultPosition=1

[3] https://www.washingtonpost.com/opinions/2022/12/05/finally-bipartisan-deal-help-dreamers-is-within-reach/; After the announcement of the bipartisan proposal, Sinema indicated that she would be leaving the Democratic party. https://www.politico.com/news/2022/12/09/sinema-arizona-senate-independent-00073216

[4] https://edition.cnn.com/2022/11/22/politics/kevin-mccarthy-homeland-security-secretary-alejandro-mayorkas-impeachment/index.html; https://www.politico.com/2022-election/results/senate/

[5] Other Christians includes any Christian not included in the white evangelical, white mainline, Black Protestant, or white and Hispanic Catholic groups. This group is multiracial and includes all Latter-day Saints, Jehovah's Witnesses, Orthodox Christians, and Hispanic Protestants.

[6] Other race Americans includes Asian Americans and Pacific Islanders, Native Americans, and any single race category that is not large enough in the survey to report independently.

[7] These results may reflect changes in wording implemented in 2022. From March 2018 until 2021, PRRI asked the following question about Dreamers: “How much do you favor or oppose allowing immigrants brought illegally to the U.S. as children to gain legal resident status?” Majorities of Americans have continuously supported this policy over this period, most recently with about two-thirds (64%) in favor. See, https://www.prri.org/research/welcoming-immigration-policies-remain-popular-but-immigration-is-not-a-critical-issue-for-most-americans/

[8] The number of cases for conservative news viewers is too small to report.

[9] The number of cases for conservative news viewers is too small to report.

[10] For an explanation of how PRRI categorizes QAnon believers, doubters, and rejecters, see our recent analysis: https://www.prri.org/spotlight/qanon-beliefs-have-increased-since-2021-as-americans-are-less-likely-to-reject-conspiracies/.

[11] There are not enough Democrats in this category to report.

[12] Each question was combined using an additive scale that was converted into a 4-point scale where a score of 1 indicates very unfavorable attitudes, 2 indicates somewhat unfavorable attitudes, 3 indicates somewhat favorable attitudes, and 4 indicates very favorable attitudes.

Prepared by PRRI Staff, January 17, 2023. (www.prri.org)

QUESTIONS FOR REFLECTION:

1. What were some key learnings for you in this survey?

2. Did you discover any surprises in this research? If so, what were they?

3. How might this research help better inform us about the diversity of attitudes in this country toward immigration?

4. What does this say about the complexity of the issue and how hard it may be to find common ground?

GLOSSARY

asylum seeker: A person who is seeking protection from persecution and serious human rights violations in their home country. According to the UN, seeking asylum is a human right.

climate migrant: A person who is forced to leave home because of climate changes.

Doctrine of Discovery: 1493 papal bull that established a religious, political, and legal justification for colonization and seizure of land not inhabited by Christians.

entry visa: A visa giving official permission to enter a country of which its bearer is not a national.

green card: Also known as a permanent resident card, it allows one to live and work in the U.S.

ICE: U.S. Immigration and Customs Enforcement.

immigrant: A person who comes to another country to live there.

immigration: Process by which individuals become permanent residents of another country.

INA: U.S. Immigration and Nationality Act.

migrant: A person who moves to a new place in order to find work or better living conditions.

refugee: A person forced to leave their country to escape persecution or natural disaster.

political refugee: A person who is forced to flee when threatened for their political beliefs.

religious refugee: A person who is forced to flee their home because of religious persecution.

sanctuary: The designation of spaces as "sanctuary" such as cities, churches, schools, etc., that seek to protect the rights of immigrants and limit the effects of immigration enforcement in communities.

UNHCR: United Nations High Commissioner for Refugees. Also refers to the UN refugee agency that works to ensure that everybody has the right to seek asylum and find safe refuge.

xenophobia: A dislike or prejudice against people from other countries.

Bibliography

Barnhill, Carla, ed. *Dialogues on the Refugee Crisis.* Minneapolis: Sparkhouse, 2018.

Bayoumi, Moustafa. *This Muslim American Life: Dispatches from the War on Terror.* New York: New York University Press, 2015.

Blitzer, Jonathan. *Trouble at the Border: How U.S. Immigration Policy and Foreign Policy Are Inextricably Linked.* London: Penguin Press, 2024.

Bouman, Stephen and Ralston Deffenbaugh. *They Are Us: Lutherans and Immigration.* Minneapolis: Fortress Press, 2020.

Butner, D. Glenn. *Jesus the Refugee: Ancient Injustice and Modern Solidarity.* Minneapolis: Fortress Press, 2023.

Choy, Catherine Ceniza. *Asian American Histories of the United States.* Boston: Beacon Press, 2022.

Diangelo, Robin. *White Fragility: Why It's So Hard for White People to Talk About Racism.* Boston: Beacon Press, 2018.

Dunbar-Oritz, Roxanne. *Not a Nation of Immigrants: Settler Colonialism, White Supremacy, and a History of Erasure and Exclusion.* Boston: Beacon Press, 2021.

Elcott, David. *Faith, Nationalism, and the Future of Liberal Democracy.* Notre Dame, IN: University of Notre Dame Press, 2021.

Goodell, Jeff. *The Heat Will Kill You First: Life and Death on a Scorched Planet.* New York: Little, Brown and Company, 2023.

Gutierrez, Elizabeth Camarillo. *My Side of the River: A Memoir.* New York: St. Martin's Press, 2024.

Hannah-Jones, Nikole, Caitlin Roper, Ilena Silverman, and Jake Silverstein, eds. *The 1619 Project: A New Origin Story.* New York: One World, 2021.

Hilton, Allen. *A House United: How the Church Can Save the World.* Minneapolis, Fortress Press, 2018.

Jodck, Darrell and William Nelson. *Embracing Diversity: Faith, Vocation and the Promise of America.* Minneapolis: Fortress Press, 2021.

Jones, Robert. *The End of White Christian America.* New York City: Simon and Schuster, 2017.

Jones, Robert. *White Too Long: The Legacy of White Supremacy in American Christianity.* New York: Simon and Schuster, 2020.

Jones, Robert. *The Hidden Roots of White Supremacy—and the Path to a Shared American Future.* New York: Simon and Schuster, 2023.

Kruse, Kevin M. and Julian E. Zelizer, eds. *Myth America: Historians Take on the Biggest Legends and Lies About Our Past.* New York: Basic Books, 2022.

Lee, Erika. *America for Americans: A History of Xenophobia in the United States*. New York: Basic Books, 2019.

Lowery, Wesley. *American Whitelash: A Changing Nation and the Cost of Progress.* New York City: Harper Collins Publishers, 2023.

Marshall, Jermaine. *Christianity Corrupted: The Scandal of White Supremacy.* Maryknoll, NY: Orbis Books, 2021.

Oliva, Alejandra. *Rivermouth: A Chronicle of Language, Faith, and Migration.* New York: Astra Publishing House, 2023.

Rouse, Rick and Paul Ingram. *The World is About to Turn: Mending a Nation's Broken Faith.* St. Louis: Chalice Press, 2020.

Sprett, Josef. *Black is a Church: Christianity and the Contours of African American Life.* New York City: Oxford University Press, 2023.

Taylor, Adam. *A More Perfect Union: A New Vision for Building the Beloved Community.* Minneapolis: Broadleaf Books, 2021.

Thurman, Howard. *Jesus and the Disinherited.* Boston: Beacon Press, 2020.

Tisby, Jemar. *How to Fight Racism: Courageous Christianity and the Journey Toward Racial Justice.* Grand Rapids, MI: Zondervan, 2021.

Tisby, Jemar,. *The Color of Compromise: The Truth About the American Church's Complicity in Racism.* Grand Rapids, MI: Zondervan, 2019.

Tobar, Hector. *Our Migrant Souls: A Meditation on Race and the Meanings and Myths of Latino.* New York: MCD—Farrar, Straus, and Giroux, 2023.

Urrea, Luis Alberto. *The Devil's Highway: A True Story*. New York: Little Brown and Company, 2004.

Wallis, Jim. *America's Original Sin: Racism, White Privilege, and the Bridge to A New America.* Grand Rapids: Brazos Press, 2017.

Wiesel, Eli. *The Night Trilogy: Night-Dawn-Day.* New York: Hill and Wang, 2008.

Immigrant Stories for Children and Youth

Badr, Nizar A. *Stepping Stones: A Refugee Family's Journey.* Victoria, B.C.:

Orca Book Publishers, 2016.

Collier, Bryan. *We Shall Overcome.* New York, Orchard Books, 2021.

Eggers, Dave. *Her Right Foot.* San Francisco: Chronicle Books LLC, 2017.

Goring, Ruth. *Adriana's Angels.* Minneapolis: Beaming Books, 2017. (Available in Spanish and in English.)

Gratz, Alan. *Refugee.* New York City: Scholastic Press, 2017.

James, Helen Foster and Virginia Shin-Mui Loh. *Paper Son: Lee's Journey to America.*

Ann Arbor, MI: Sleeping Bear Press, 2013.

Mills, Deborah, Alfredo Alva, and Claudia Navaro. *La Fontera: My Journey with Popa.* Concord, MA: Barefoot Books, 2018.

Morales, Yuri and Luisa Uribe. *Areli is a Dreamer: A True Story.* New York: Penguin Random House, 2018.

Morales, Yuyi. *Dreamers.* New York: Penguin Random House, 2018.

Tang, Marie. *Yuna's Cardboard Castles.* Minneapolis: Beaming Books, 2023.

Tuininga, Josh. *We Are Not Strangers.* New York: Abrams Books, 2023.

Williams, Karen Lynn. *Four Feet, Two Sandals.* Grand Rapids, MI: Eerdmans, 2007.

Williams, Mary and R. Gregory Christie. *Brothers in Hope: The Story of the Lost Boys of* Sudan. New York: Lee and Low Books, 2005.

Yaccarino, Dan. *All the Way to America: The Story of a Big Italian Family.* New York: Alfred A. Knopf Publishers, 2011.

Resources on Christian Nationalism

Alberta, Tim. *The Kingdom, the Power, and the Glory: American Evangelicals in an Age of Extremism.* New York: Harper Collins Publishers, 2023.

Berg, Thomas. *Religious Liberty in a Polarized Age.* Grand Rapids, MI: Wm. B. Eerdmans Publishing, 2023.

Boyd, Gregory. *The Myth of a Christian Nation: How the Quest for Political Power Is Destroying the Church.* Grand Rapids: Zondervan, 2005

Cooper-White, Pamela. *The Psychology of Christian Nationalism: Why People Are Drawn In and How to Talk Across the Divide.* Minneapolis: Fortress Press, 2022.

Gorski, Philip and Samuel Perry. *The Flag and the Cross: White Christian Nationalism and the Threat to American Democracy.* New York: Oxford University Press, 2022.

Gushee, David P. *Defending Democracy from Its Christian Enemies.* Grand Rapids: Wm. B. Eerdmans Publishing, 2023.

Hendricks Jr., Obery. *Christians Against Christianity: How Right-Wing Evangelicals Are Destroying Our Nation and Our Faith.* Boston: Beacon Press, 2021.

Kaylor, Brian and Beau Underwood. *Baptizing America: How Mainline Protestants Helped Build Christian Nationalism.* St. Louis: Chalice Press, 2024.

Miller, Paul. *The Religion of American Greatness: What's Wrong with Christian Nationalism.* Westmont, IL: InterVarsity Press Academic, 2022.

Onishi, Bradley. *Preparing for War: The Extremist History of White Christian Nationalism and What Comes Next.* Minneapolis, Fortress Press, 2022.

Perry, Samuel and Philip Gorski. *The Flag and the Cross: White Christian Nationalism and the Threat to Democracy.* New York: Oxford University Press, 2022.

Seidel, Andrew. *The Founding Myth: Why Christian Nationalism Is Un-American.* New York: Sterling Press, 2019.

Stevens, Stuart. *The Conspiracy to End America: Five Ways My Old Party is Driving Our Democracy to Autocracy.* New York: Hachette Book Group, 2023.

Stewart, Kathrine. *The Power Worshippers: Inside the Dangerous Rise of Religious Nationalism.* New York: Bloomsbury Publishing, 2019.

Taylor, Matthew. *The Violent Take It By Force: The Christian Movement Threatening Our Democracy.* Minneapolis: Broadleaf Books, 2024.

Wallis, Jim. *The False White Gospel: Rejecting Christian Nationalism, Reclaiming True Faith, and Refounding Democracy.* New York City: St. Martin's Press, 2024.

Whitehead, Andrew. *American Idolatry: How Christian Nationalism Betrays the Gospel and Threatens the Church.* Grand Rapids: Brazos Press, 2023.

Whitehead, Andrew and Samuel Perry. *Taking America Back for God: Christian Nationalism in the United States.* New York: Oxford University Press, 2020.

Wilkerson, Isabel. *Caste: The Origins of Our Discontents.* New York, Random House, 2020.

Wright, N.T. and Michael F. Bird. *Jesus and the Powers: Christian Political Witness in an Age of Totalitarian Terror and Dysfunctional Democracies.* Grand Rapids: Zondervan, 2024.

Zahnd, Brian. *Postcards from Babylon: The Church in American Exile.* Sacramento: Spello Press, 2019.